SHAPING YOUR LIFE

The Power of Creative Imagery

by
Laurel Jan Fuller
D.D., B.A.

SOM Publishing
Windyville, Missouri 65783

Other titles by Laurel Jan Fuller

- **Total Recall**

An Introduction to Past Life & Health Readings

© January, 1994
by the School of Metaphysics No. 100148

Front Cover Art by Sharka Glet

ISBN: 0-944386-14-8

Library of Congress Catalogue Number pending

PRINTED IN THE UNITED STATES OF AMERICA

If you desire to learn more about the research and
teachings in this book, write to School of Metaphysics,
National Headquarters, Windyville, Missouri 65783.
Or call 417-345-8411.

Contents

*I dedicate this book to my parents
who taught me to imagine
by reading to me, telling stories, playing music,
and encouraging my love of books.*

"Our life is shaped by our mind;
we become what we think.
Suffering follows an evil thought
as the wheels of a cart
follow the oxen that draw it.
Our life is shaped by our mind;
we become what we think.
Joy follows a pure thought
like a shadow that never leaves."
— Dhammapada, Twin Verses, v. 1-2

"As irrigators lead water where they want,
as archers make their arrows straight,
as carpenters carve wood,
the wise shape their minds."
—Dhammapada, The Wise, v. 80

Preface

It was beautiful sunny day. Jay, Rick, Sheila and Deborah were burning piles of brush that they had cleared from a wild tract of land in mid-Missouri. They were pioneers, removing the brushy tangle of scrub oak so the area would be tamed for fields and pasture. Suddenly, the wind picked up. The pile of brush that was burning nestled in a small valley immediately burst into a rapidly spreading fire.

Tiny five-foot tall Deborah screamed and grabbed a shovel to try to pound out the flames. Jay and Rick stood there, paralyzed for a second, wondering whether they had time to run to get help. Sheila rapidly assessed the situation. She respected the tremendous power and swiftness of fire and knew that they had to respond at once. She could see that physical manpower would not stop the flames which were escalating in size and speed. By the time the local volunteer fire department arrived from the outlying country areas, the fire would have already consumed half of the thousand-acre property. The fire was rapidly spreading toward the woods and once it reached the trees they would never be able to control it. Sheila had to do something. She and many other people had worked long and hard to buy this land and to tend it for the purpose of building a spiritual community. She felt sick to her stomach foreseeing the possibility of one small fire spreading to destroy a thousand acres.

Sheila said to herself, "If I really am a mental creator, I can stop this." She quickly centered herself and said, "Wind! I command you to be still." She visualized the wind calming down, the fire subsiding, and the brush pile burning itself out in a small area. Within seconds the wind died down. The fire ceased running rampant and Sheila contained it in one place. Deborah, Jay and Rick stopped their frantic and futile attempts to beat out the flames and gaped in wonder. Then they all cheered and hugged one another with joy.

This is a true story. It is not a fairy tale, nor allegory, nor fabricated fable. Sheila is a friend of mine who had been studying metaphysics and practicing concentration and visualization for about five years when this incident occurred. It seems like a miracle to be able to stop the wind, and yet, this miracle occurred in the modern twentieth century. Through the power of creative imagery, directed with concentration and will, one woman stopped a fire and saved a newly-forming community from vast destruction.

People throughout the world use visualization on a daily basis, to create wondrous projects, to build cities, to compose inspiring music. People use visualization to heal themselves of cancer, AIDS, and other life-threatening diseases. Others use it in emergencies — a 120-pound woman has been known to lift a car by herself to save her child trapped underneath. Creative imagery has been used throughout the ages by inventors, scientists, and innovators to develop new ways of life: the telephone, electrical light bulb, radio, television, automobile, and airplane all resulted from the imagination and will of their creators.

Now *you* can learn about the power of your creative mind. You can learn how to design your life dreams, how to change annoying habits, how to improve relationships. You can learn how to draw upon the wellspring of creativity which is at the very essence of your being. You can truly have anything you desire in the mental, emotional and spiritual realm by developing your imagination and will power.

This is your life. It is yours to create, to fashion, to shape and to make according to your innermost urge to become your highest and best Self. When you are giving from the place within you which is your most excellent Self, the world will be a better place for all.

PART I

Changing Your Life

Changing Habits

After sixteen years of being a heavy (two packs a day) smoker, I quit and can report happily that I have never touched a cigarette in the past four years, nor have I gained weight, nor do I regret it, nor do I miss smoking. The secret to changing addictive habits lies, not in the exercise of will power, but in the effective use of visualization. Every physical habit starts with a thought. At one time, I had imagined myself being a smoker and practiced a particular image along with the physical activity of smoking. As I created a strong thought-form image of smoking, my body also became accustomed to the nicotine. So when the time came to quit, I had to change not only the visualized image of myself as a smoker, but also the physical condition of addiction.

As you have probably heard, to change a habit you must want to do it. How do you create a desire for something you are going to leave? When you are attached to an idea it becomes a part of you, and to lose it means losing a part of your identity. It is tricky, therefore, to create a different image that will involve productive gain rather than deprivation, denial, and loss. For a long time I tried unsuccessfully to quit smoking, because the image in my mind of quitting was like seeing a cigarette with a red "don't" line through it. Every time I thought about quitting, I thought about cigarettes until my mind was filled with the thought of smoking incessantly!

The first step in creating a desire for change is to identify what the habit represents. In my case, I had to remember when I first started formulating the idea of smoking. I remembered clearly when I was fifteen years old having an older sister whom I admired and who represented maturity to me. She smoked, my parents had smoked when I was a child, and although they no longer smoked by the time I was fifteen, my earliest images of adulthood incorporated smoking. I read the magazines that showed glamorous pictures of worldly women holding cigarettes, and I had seen old movies with Lauren Bacall looking sexy and sophisticated expectantly waiting for Humphrey Bogart to light her cigarette. So in my adolescence I associated smoking with the idea of being mature, adult, sophisticated, sexy, alluring, and womanly.

I remember buying my first pack of cigarettes and going to my room, locking the door, sitting in front of the mirror and practicing holding the cigarette, practicing inhaling it. At first the smoke was acrid and tasted terrible, but my desire for maturity and sophistication was so strong I was able to keep inhaling until I had overcome my body's resistance to the poison. As I practiced cultivating this new image, I became attached to the cigarette as a symbol of my new-found and developing adulthood. Years later, as an adult, the thought which originated the desire to smoke was not so strong, but I still found myself smoking more during the times when I felt my authority challenged. It was enlightening to explore these early memories and to discover the thought-image which generated the action of picking up a cigarette.

As I developed the habit of smoking, I related other images with the action of picking up a cigarette. Moments of intimacy, after sexual encounters, sharing secrets over a cup of coffee, long talks on the phone, all of these events became associated with smoking. As I explored these connections, I found out that I had been using cigarettes as a form of protection. When I was revealing my deepest "private" self, I would light a cigarette to keep myself at a distance from the person with whom I was becoming intimate. Smoking cigarettes was a way to repress my emotions.

I also used cigarettes to procrastinate. Waiting for a bus, lingering after a meal, between projects at work, I would smoke. I often drank a cup of coffee and smoked a cigarette or two to start my day — first at home, and again when I arrived at work. Lighting a cigarette was a way to literally kill time. When I was being indecisive or non-committal or insecure about what to do next, I would think, "I'll do this after I have a cigarette" and thus put off the decision for a few more minutes.

In addition, after years of smoking my body had become addicted to the nicotine. So the decision to quit smoking was a multi-faceted one which involved re-thinking many activities in my life, becoming conscious of thoughts that had been submerged in unconsciousness, and disciplining my physical senses and physical body. It was scary to think about giving up my protection, giving up this constant companion, giving up the cigarettes that I clung to when I was being insecure. Cigarettes had infiltrated every area of my life and anywhere I went — at home, in my car, at work, in bed — there were stimuli to draw my attention to my attachment. I needed a positive, attractive reason to quit smoking because I had actually developed a sixteen-year *relationship* with cigarettes!

The desire to cause this habit to change originated, not from fear of cancer or disease, but from hating the slavery to which I had subjected myself. I realized that I had become a slave to cigarettes. The relationship that at one time seemed so appealing was now abusive and masochistic. At two o'clock in the morning, undressed and almost ready for bed, I had found myself frantically searching the house for a cigarette, and if I could not find one, rather than saying, "Oh, well, I'll get some tomorrow," I'd get dressed and go out and buy some. Or I would stoop to rummaging through the trash for a long "butt" which was still smokable — looking and feeling like a common bum! Every place I went, I would look for the areas where smoking was permitted, I was always checking to make sure I had my cigarettes with me, and I would gauge time by how long it had been since I had had a cigarette. Much of my attention was consumed by thinking about smoking.

In every other area of my life I was striving for mastery. As a serious student of metaphysics, I had practiced concentration exercises for years. I had practiced a weekly discipline of eating only fruit to be in command of my body. I sat still for hours in meditation. I was teaching people how to control their lives, teaching them how powerful their minds were, and here I was being enslaved by cigarettes! This idea was offensive to me, for it conflicted with everything I believed and the principles on which I based my life. I do not like hypocritical behavior in others, and here I was being a hypocrite myself. The urge to be a good example to my students and to live up to my own ideals motivated me to form a new desire.

I decided that I was tired of being a slave and I wanted to be a master. This was the positive thought-form image I created to replace the old one: being the master of my life, my circumstances, my thoughts, and my senses. I imaged myself having command of my attention and having command of mySelf. Now, because the addiction to the nicotine was strong, I still had to deal with the physical withdrawal. I used various methods to help with this. I bought some herbal tablets at a health food store which contained an herb called lobelia, which helps reduce the craving for nicotine without creating a new addiction. I read books which said that the actual physical craving for nicotine lasts about sixty seconds. When I felt the irritating sensation of crawling out of my skin and being immeasurably agitated and restless, I would breathe deeply, go for a walk, drink lots of water, direct my attention elsewhere, and indeed in a minute or so the most acute physical discomfort was gone. When I was tempted to pick up a cigarette, especially when no one was around and I could rationalize that no one would know, I'd ask myself, "Laurel, what do you want? Do you want to be the slave or do you want to be the master?" Every time I considered this question carefully, for I realized that I did not *have* to quit. I could still smoke if I wanted to, but if I smoked I would once again be enslaved. And so I would answer, "I want to be the master." Every time I practiced mastery I was proud of myself, and every day at the close of the day I would mark off how many days I had accomplished this mastery. Every time I was tempted to smoke just one drag, I would think about the amount of time and energy I had already invested in this change and that I wanted the investment to pay off. If I smoked even one drag I knew I would have to start all over again from the beginning and I wanted to add on to what I had already invested.

Gradually, I became less attached to the *idea* of being a smoker and more and more attached to the pride and security that came from knowing that *I was the master* of my mind and body. In time, the physical cravings lessened. As I gave conscious attention to my thoughts and *why* I craved cigarettes at certain times, I also learned how I had used cigarettes to protect myself from being vulnerable in intimate moments and to pretend to be mature when I doubted my authority. I practiced being inwardly calm, learning to receive and to give rather than reaching for a smoke. These experiences were very enriching, for I built strength and confidence in areas where I had used cigarettes as a crutch.

I know that because I practiced consciously changing my image and cultivating a new, productive, powerful image to replace the one I had been attached to, this change is a permanent one. I do not miss cigarettes, and I never replaced that habit with another one such as gum chewing or eating compulsively. The change was in my thoughts and attitudes, not in the physical behavior alone. "Behavior modification" works when there is conscious attention given to the thoughts that are causing the behavior and those *thoughts* are changed with visualization. Changing the behavior with the thoughts staying the same leads to new compulsive behavior with a different object of attachment.

Another way to use visualization to change habits is for creating the kind of body you desire. Most women in this country have the idea that they are fat, even when they are remarkably skinny. Hopefully one day we will learn to respect and appreciate the female form with its curves, but for the time being models are depicted as skinny, with perfectly chiseled features that reveal no body fat. Commercials abound that tell us that we will be happy when we are pencil thin, and that food makes us fat. At the same time, we are taught that certain foods will soothe us, our mothers feed us to make us be quiet when we are babies, we turn to ice cream and chocolate to assuage our emotional upsets, and then hate ourselves for eating!

I knew a young woman who battled overweight throughout her childhood, adolescence, and early adulthood and finally conquered the "fat demon" through practicing creative imagery. Rachel was very intelligent and shy. She loved to read and would spend long hours inside the house, devouring books.

Her sports-loving mother kept telling Rachel, "You're not athletic" and the child believed it. When she did venture outside to play kickball or softball, she held the image that she was awkward and clumsy, so she was picked last to be on the neighborhood kids' team. This reinforced her dislike for her body and discomfort with the idea of physical activity.

Rachel's mother was health conscious and served meals that were low in fat and sugar. She had waged her own battles with overweight and was afraid of foods that were "fattening." Thus, Rachel grew up with the idea that food had power over her, that she would gain weight from eating any food with sugar or fat in it. She denied herself some of the foods she enjoyed, like chocolate and ice cream, and then in fits of rebellion, she would gorge herself with large quantities of both. Rachel used food as a form of comfort, when she was sad, or anxious, or lonely. She also used eating as a way of asserting her will: "no one's going to tell me what I shouldn't eat!"

Rachel hated having to worry about every bit of food she put into her mouth. She hated being at odds with her body. She wanted to enjoy eating instead of feeling guilty about it, and she wanted to like her body rather than viewing it as her enemy. She had a friend who was skinny, who ate like a horse and stayed thin. Her friend was always saying, "I can eat anything I want and never gain an ounce," and this was true! Rachel was always dieting and as she listened to her thoughts and fears about gaining weight, she found herself thinking, "If I even look at a piece of chocolate cake I gain five pounds." She started watching the people around her and discovered that those who were lean thought of themselves as slim; those who were always afraid of gaining weight talked and thought of themselves as chubby, chunky, or fat.

"I wonder what it would be like to be thin?" she pondered. This was a new thought for her! Previously, she had tried to keep her weight down, to stem the tide of increasing weight gain. She had imaged herself being clumsy, awkward, and uncomfortable with her physical form. But now she started imagining how it would feel to move easily and gracefully. She stood in front of a mirror with her clothes off and examined her body. It wasn't so bad, but, like a sculptor with a critical eye she pictured how her body would look if she sculpted it differently — if her stomach were flat, if her thighs were firm. She tightened her muscles to define their shape and viewed her body as she wanted it to be. As she looked in the mirror she began to develop some objectivity — this body was not *her,* it was a body. So even though her body might have some extra fat, that didn't mean that *Rachel* was fat. Rachel had never before realized how pervasive was her dislike for herself and her image of *fat* — lazy, slothful, sluggish, awkward, unable to coordinate with the rest of the world.

Rachel started to develop a new respect for herself. She eyed this body's bone structure and began to appreciate its strength and balance and proportion. She decided to learn how to get acquainted with her body and to cooperate with it rather than fighting it. Every time she moved, whether it was bending down to pick up a pencil, walking up a flight of stairs or lifting a sack of flour she visualized her muscles being toned, her body tight and firm. She found out that her thoughts *could* command her body. This stimulated her to speed up the process with exercise. She experimented with walking, bicycle riding, swimming, aerobics, and yoga and found that she enjoyed walking and stretching with yoga, so she incorporated these activities into her life. By visualizing her body becoming fit, toned, graceful, and fluid, even a minimal amount of physical exercise produced tremendous results.

As Rachel harmonized with her body and learned to cooperate with its need for movement, she also began paying attention to the process of eating. She visualized food nourishing her body, being used efficiently by all the cells and organs, causing them to sing with health and vigor. She imaged the waste products being sloughed off and carried away and drank lots of water to facilitate the process. She appreciated the food and started giving her full attention to the tastes and textures rather than sneaking food with guilt or grabbing it with rebellion. She practiced listening to herself to choose the foods that her body needed. When she just shoved food into her mouth without thinking, Rachel might eat chocolate when her physical system needed protein or choose salty chips when her body needed water. She became more attentive to her body's needs and requirements. She imaged her body perking up with renewed energy and life, the cells saying "thank you for feeding me well." By loving her meals, chewing the food, enjoying its flavor and feel, Rachel found that she was satisfied eating smaller quantities. She learned to more accurately interpret the cravings and signals from her appetite.

This process helped Rachel to develop some awareness of her motivation for eating. At times she ate when she was physically hungry. But often she ate because she was lonely and wanted comfort. Sometimes she found she would turn to the refrigerator when she was angry and suppressing the anger. She started to keep a journal in which she wrote down the thoughts she associated with the food she ate, and discovered that when she ate out of defiance or anger or to soothe a hurt, the food tended to settle on her body as a fat barrier from the cold, cruel world. Self examination brought her to the discovery that some of the foods she craved represented something else. It wasn't so much the taste of chocolate she craved, it was the comfort it represented. She remembered that her mother used to give her cake on special occasions, so she associated it with being good and being loved. She also remembered feeling deprived because her friends could eat candy any time they wanted, and she was restricted about the amount she could eat. So sometimes she would go overboard eating sweets to prove that she could do what she wanted in life. She had had a boyfriend at one time who badgered her to lose weight, and some of her dieting was an attempt to please him. So when she was angry with him, she ate more to defy him, and even after the relationship ended she resorted to food as a statement of self-assertion.

As she learned to discriminate when she was eating to satisfy an inner need, she began to image different methods of fulfilling those needs. For example, Rachel had always wanted to write a book, but every time she attempted it, her mind was flooded with self-deprecating messages she had accepted and practiced, "You'll never be able to complete anything you start. You won't amount to much." Instead of approaching the typewriter, she would walk over to the refrigerator and eat until she felt better. Changing the behavior meant changing the accompanying thoughts. She started thinking loving, positive thoughts about herself. She reminded herself of how she had started respecting her body with exercise and gave herself a compliment. She set goals to commit herself to writing for a given length of time each day. As she acted on these goals, she was less inclined to feed her body for comfort because she was feeding her soul with productive activity.

Visualization helped Rachel to enjoy food and to end her "love-hate" relationship with it, developing a more healthy respect for her body and its needs. She quit eating in secret and trying to hide her desire for food, which had only perpetuated the self-hatred and compulsive behavior. She also developed some pride in herself through appreciating physical movement and toning her body so that it could more readily respond to her desires for action. Because she used visualization to change her *thinking,* Rachel no longer had to turn to eating to find satisfaction. She visualized herself communicating with people whom she felt controlled her rather than rebelling by stuffing herself with food, and then she practiced new communication skills. She imaged a new Rachel who was strong, secure, productive, happy, healthy, in control of herself and her world, and easily able to respond to life's challenges.

If you wonder how it is possible to use mental imaging to change the dense physical matter of your body, consider the idea that the nature of the physical world is change. The molecules which make up the physical body are a whirling bundle of activity. As such, they are fluid, changeable, and responsive to your mental direction. Have you ever thought about what happened to your five-year-old body? Did it disappear? If not, where is it now? The answer is this: your five-year-old body has changed. The body you use now still has two hands, two feet, face, trunk, and so forth. But it is a structure that has evolved from the one you inhabited when you were five years old. Your body evolved as you evolved. As you imaged yourself being six years old, your body changed. Similarly, as you image yourself being lithe, lean, and fit, and toned, your body will follow suit.

If this still seems unreal, think about a time when you were facing an important goal or project and you were so keyed up about it you had trouble going to sleep. Even though your body may have required rest, because your mind was still active your body stayed in motion. Probably you remained energized until you had accomplished your goal (completed the important meeting, went on the anticipated date) and then, when it was over, you fell asleep exhausted. How did this happen? Your mental alertness, the desire to complete the project and your thoughts on the expected event, caused your metabolism to remain active and your body stayed energized. Or, think about a time when you were depressed. You had no goals, nothing to which you could look forward. Maybe you even dreaded going to work in the morning. When your alarm rang, you felt exhausted even though you may have slept well over eight hours. In this case, your attention was on avoiding your day. You did not want to face the events, so your body slowed down in response, ready for sleep. The sleep was not needed for rest; it was an escape from life.

These are two examples of how your body can respond to the thoughts you create. There are others, and if you explore your memory you will probably recognize times when you have commanded your body to follow your mental direction. Believe in your power to create with thought, and you will change your life for the better. Creative imaging can be used to change whatever habits you desire. Whether it is smoking, eating, gum chewing or nail biting, the process is the same. Remember that to change addictive behaviors you must draw out and face the images that initiated the behavior in the first place. If you have difficulty with this, counseling may be beneficial to aid you to develop Self awareness. Once you have identified the causal thought, that is, the image you created when you first started practicing the addictive behavior and which you have repeated since then, you are on your way to creating new, productive, healthy images. When you follow with the practice of healthy behaviors, you have productive change.

Self Image

"You are as you think you are." You have probably heard this statement, but have you understood its implications? A couple of years ago I worked as an assistant editor for a medical publisher in St. Louis. This publisher specialized in plastic surgery textbooks and reference books, and I had the opportunity to work on a book about rhinoplasty, plastic surgery of the nose. One of the plastic surgeons who contributed to this book did a study and found that the best patients for plastic surgery were those with a good self image and objectively severe deformities. The worst patients where those with a low self image and relatively minor deformities. The surgeon had discovered that an unfortunate number of patients came to a doctor expecting that he would "fix" their nose and thus "fix" their life. They found, after the surgery, that with a different nose they still had the same difficulties finding a job, creating healthy relationships, being happy and wealthy. The physical change did not cause an inner change. On the contrary, oftentimes they were even *more* depressed after the surgery because that was their hope which soon gave way to despair.

One chapter in the book that was especially distressing to me was the one on "ethnic" noses. The book illustrated before and after photographs of people who had rhinoplasty in an attempt to makeover their racial or ethnic heritage. In one case, a beautiful woman with a classic "Jewish" nose had hers changed, the rounded edge taken off and replaced with a ski-lift curve. After the surgery she would not leave her house, because she couldn't bear to look in the mirror with the "artificial" nose facing her. Her difficulty was not the nose, it was her image of herself. She had learned to hate her Jewish heritage from having been "victimized" by anti-Semitic remarks. Never having resolved the core issue — her own sense of worthlessness and powerlessness — changing her physical body only heightened the conflict. She had destroyed a part of herself physically to match the self-hatred she already experienced.

Your physical features may be plain or pretty, but beauty does not come from physical causes. We have all seen women who pile on makeup and get their hair done and still appear unattractive. And we have seen people who, with little adornment, radiate an inner beauty that makes them irresistibly appealing. What causes this inner light to shine? What causes this beauty? Philosophers have debated this question through the ages. The poet John Keats, in his "Ode on a Grecian Urn" determined that "Beauty is truth, truth beauty, — that is all/ Ye know on earth, and all ye need to know." Beauty is an understanding and expression of truth, and we consider someone or something beautiful when they are fully giving from their innermost self. When a person follows their innermost urge to give, when they know who they are and are willing to share themselves with others, they are very beautiful. This is why we think a woman who has just given birth is beautiful — she has offered a precious gift to the world. When one has completed a project, when they are involved in a creative endeavor, when they give a speech and share their deep insights and feelings, they are beautiful.

How we image ourselves is a powerful determinant of how we experience our lives. When we focus on our talents, skills, and wisdom and give freely and generously, we think we are beautiful and we appear beautiful. We improve the world in which we live because we continually add something beneficial anywhere we go. We are happy, because we know that our presence makes a productive difference to the people we touch. When we deny our worth, when we look at what we think are our faults, we appear tired, old, ugly, and unattractive. We take from our environment, trying to get attention from other people rather than giving ourselves to them to enrich their lives. We become defensive, depressed, and sullen because we drain those around us.

To discover how you think of yourself, you can make a Self Image Inventory. On a sheet of paper, write your full name, then number 1 to 25. After each number, write "I am" and then finish the sentence with a word or phrase that describes you. Don't stop to think, let your mind go, and write the first thought that comes to mind. You may have some physical descriptions, such as "I am tall," "I am skinny," "I am white"; you may have some phrases that describe your attitudes, "I am lonely," "I am honest." You may have some statements that describe your skills and abilities: "I am creative," "I am a good writer," etc. Once you have finished your list, look it over and determine which qualities and attributes are productive. These are your "toolbox" of talents that you have available to use to create your Ideal Self. Then look at the unproductive or negative items on the list. Decide how you want to change those handicaps. For example, if you put "I am depressed" you could change that to "I am energetic with goals that inspire me" or something to that effect. This Self Image Inventory will help you to discover where you are in your awareness of yourself and will provide a direction for you to create the changes you desire.

The next step is to practice being who you want to be. Once you have decided what you want to change, visualize or image the Ideal Self you want to become. For many people, this is the most difficult aspect of visualization. They have no difficulty creating images of physical objects or circumstances, but their self image is so ingrained they may have a hard time creating a new image. If this is the case for you, you can use a technique called "acting as if." For this technique, you must choose someone you know or have seen who exhibits the qualities you desire. Then, "act as if" you are that person. This will transport you out of your imagined limitation and you will transcend into a new, creative reality. You may even want to choose several people who demonstrate the qualities you want to build and combine these people into a composite role model.

For example, when I first started practicing metaphysics I was very shy. I had been shy ever since I was a child and it was a strongly embedded thought-form image. All my life people had told me I was shy, my teachers in school commented on it, my parents referred to me as quiet and shy, and I identified strongly with this idea. On a number of occasions I forced myself to attend parties and other social gatherings where there would be a crowd of people, but I was very uncomfortable and awkward because of my shyness. Friends often urged me to go out more, but I insisted that I preferred staying home with a book. Changing this shyness was not really something I *wanted* to change, it was something I thought I "should" change.

Finally, I started to think that this shyness had disadvantages. As I learned more about metaphysics I wanted to share my discoveries with other people, and it was a handicap to be so afraid of people. At first, I didn't have a positive desire image, but I did have a motivation — I was tired of being uncomfortable around people. I had also been told that is was selfish of me to hold myself back from communicating because there were other people around me who wanted to know the things I knew. I didn't much like the idea I was selfish! Still, I had so strongly identified with being shy it was hard for me to imagine being anything else. I had a couple of friends who were outgoing, gregarious, funny, talkative people. I would think to myself, "I'm just not like that." So I used this thought to my advantage. When I went to a lecture or to a party or some other event in which there were a lot unfamiliar people, I would pretend to be Margie or Jennifer, my friends who were outgoing. I would "act as if" I were they. And, rather easily, I found myself laughing, smiling, talking, initiating conversations with strangers. In the beginning, I didn't imagine *myself* being like that, but I did imagine what *they* would be like in a social setting. I imagined that they would very easily go up to anyone whether they knew them or not, they would be interested in the other person, ask them questions, initiate conversation. When I was in that setting I would pretend I was one of them and visualized the action. Then I followed through with the actual practice. Gradually, I found that I was becoming like Margie and Jennifer. I found that I was becoming friendly, outgoing, and talkative. It was as if I had "tricked" myself into practicing qualities I didn't image myself having. But because it was I who was doing the visualizing, it was I who was creating a new image!

This technique of "acting as if" will get you started to practice any productive quality you desire. You can "act as if" you are confident while you are building a belief in yourself; you can "act as if" you are a leader while you are learning to develop leadership skills, you can "act as if" you are a good singer while you are educating yourself on the use of your voice. It is important that in this process you *visualize* the desired quality and action, *image* yourself being the way you desire to be, for if you habitually image the old way of thinking and behaving, the physical activity will not produce the results you desire.

For example, there was a young man named Lou whose father was the owner of a successful business. When Lou graduated from business college, he was hired as the manager of one of the departments in his father's business. Lou was capable, intelligent, and bright and his father believed that he could use this position to gain the experience to become an excellent leader. Lou, however, was very insecure. He imaged himself as a child always seeking his father's approval. He was convinced that the only reason he was hired for the job was because he was the boss's son — it never occurred to him that he had any worthwhile qualifications. Because he wanted to please his father, Lou accepted the job but was constantly defensive, on guard in case anyone should ridicule him for being the "baby boss's son." He imitated other department managers by acting bossy and giving orders, but in his mind and in his imagination he was still a kid. As a result, his fear came to pass. He was faced with a rebellious department and employees who asked, "Why should we listen to you? Just because your old man got you this job?"

Lou had difficulty because he only *pretended* to be a leader rather than *imagining* himself that way. Pretending is imitating behavior without changing the way of thinking. Lou imaged himself as inadequate, inferior, inexperienced, and begging for approval. His outer behavior was bossy without any foundation based on experience or purposeful thinking. Had he used creative imagery, Lou could have imagined himself making wise judgments. When difficult situations arose with the employees, Lou could have imagined the outcome of various choices on his part and could have discussed these options with his supervisor. In this way, he would have gained experience in learning how to think as a manager, how to make judgments that would keep everyone's best interest in mind. Then he could have acted on these choices with the intent of gaining further understanding and experience. By using his supervisor for feedback rather than approval, Lou would have grown into a true understanding of authority based on his own knowledge and experience. Lou needed to image himself being an adult, thinking as a leader, and drawing upon his own inner resources to cause a change inwardly and outwardly.

In creating a new self image, listen to the words you use to describe yourself. Do you say, "I'm only a sophomore," "I've only had two years experience" or do you say, "I'm already a sophomore," "I've had a full two years' experience"? The difference is the pride you take in your accomplishments. Never take yourself for granted! Always respect where you are in your development, the steps you have taken and the ones you are currently taking to achieve your ideals. What you envision you can have, and this includes the highest ideals you image for yourself. Describe yourself with honest self respect and pride, practice *living* the ideals you espouse, be the moral character you desire to be, and you will find that others will treat you as you treat yourself.

The image you hold of yourself will affect your demeanor, your posture, even your physical appearance. I know a woman who illustrates this fact. When she is productive, creative, and happy, she has a beautiful and warm smile that radiates throughout her whole being. She is strikingly attractive in person and in photographs. But when she is being selfish or lazy, she becomes very angry. She blames other people or conditions for her plight, and her face registers the hatred she holds for her life at these times. You can hardly tell that she is the same person! Her face becomes hard and ugly. You probably know people like this. You may notice that when a person is depressed, they hunch their shoulders and walk with a slow, shuffling gait. When one is interested in life, they walk tall and have a spring in their step.

In many instances you can observe yourself to see how

your self image affects your choices and understanding of creation.   When you are budgeting your money to make the greatest use of your resources, do you think of yourself as wise by using the physical world to its fullest, or do you think of yourself as "broke"? Do you shop at second-hand stores because you enjoy creating interesting outfits from recycled energy, being imaginative as you respect the environment?   Or do you shop at second-hand stores because you think you can't afford anything else?   The same action will produce different results in your consciousness according to your intention.   When you create a strong, positive, productive self image *any* action in which you become involved will reflect the pride and integrity you emanate.   When you create a defeated, victimized, "poor" self image, you will show that, too.   You will think the world is against you and that you never get your due.   In fact, in either case, your own thoughts determine the results.   It is your choice; exercise your free will with wisdom.

Hold your head high and display the confidence, the growth, the intelligence and creativity that you have.   You will find that people flock to you, you will find that you have the "Midas touch" — everything will turn to gold in your hands. You will create the fondest dreams and greatest aspirations you have because you are identifying with the creative intelligence that is the *real you.*

Exploring Your Talents

Did you ever watch a dancer on television, admiring their grace and poise and fluidity, and think to yourself, "What would I give to dance like that!" Or perhaps you envied a great musician, or sportscaster, or basketball player. Did you then think, "I'll do it!" or did you breathe a sigh and say, "I could never do that. I'm such a klutz."

Either way, you are activating the formative power of your mind. Henry Ford said, "Think you can, think you can't. Either way you're right!" When you form an image in your mind, all the forces of the universe follow the command of your mind. Since you are the director of your life, since your thoughts determine the quality of your existence, doesn't it make sense to image what you *want*?

Anyone who is successful will tell you that they create a strong thought-form image of how they want to be and then practice, practice, practice. Arsenio Hall, who is rapidly becoming the number one late night television talk show host, tapes his shows and then watches them two or three times to observe his actions and demeanor. Then, he visualizes how he wants to improve so that he can practice that the following night. Arnold Schwarzenegger, world champion body builder, has said that the most important element of shaping the body is forming a detailed image in the mind. He visualizes the muscles becoming the size and shape he desires as he "pumps iron" and creates a clear mental image of strength and endurance as he exercises. Dancers watch other dancers, musicians listen to performances of music over and over to hear every nuance of the piece they will be playing. They include in their mental imagery what the music will sound like as well as how they will manipulate the instrument. Basketball, baseball, and football players visualize themselves performing on the field. First, they create a strong mental image and next, they practice the physical activity. With the combination of mental imagery and physical practice, these people accelerate their progress.

One of the benefits of this mental imagery is that it helps to alleviate nervousness. Anyone who desires to excel will experience anxiety, nervousness, or agitation prior to an important performance. This is the outpush of the emotions. Any time a visualized thought form is ready to be birthed into physical existence, there is an accompanying expression of emotion. In fact, the purpose of the emotional level of consciousness is to push thoughts out of the inner, subconscious mind into the conscious, physical level of existence. One can either react to this emotion by fighting it, trying to stuff the emotion back and pretending to be "cool" (thus creating even more anxiety which will explode!) or cooperate with it. Cooperating with the emotion means using the enthusiasm, excitement, and thrill of anticipation. Turn stage fright into a powerful expression of emotional energy!

When you have visualized yourself performing as you desire, whether on stage or on the sports field, or in the corporate boardroom, you are prepared. This mental preparation is just as important as the physical preparations you make. By visualizing yourself being as you desire, you will perfect *in your mind* the steps you need to take, so that you actually need less physical practice time. This causes you to become much more efficient and directed in your life.

It is important in this mental practice time to create a clearly defined ideal which involves your whole being. Image not only how you desire to present yourself on the *outside,* but also image how you desire to give of yourself, the qualities you want to exude, how you want to feel, the thoughts you want to be thinking and creating. This complete image of yourself, from the inside out, will cause success. Visualize *who you want to be* as well as visualizing how you want to appear. This is the difference between using imagination and pretending. Most children are expert pretenders. They will dress up in Mom's shoes or Dad's hat and pretend to be an adult. But, they still think like children. When they start learning how to be responsible, making decisions for themselves, thinking in an adult way how to be productive, they begin to become adults. You can put on the air of being confident while inside you are quaking. You can imagine how *other people* will see you and still feel unprepared. You want to image *yourself* being how you want to be in your mind and thoughts and intentions. This is how you will cause your outer expression to be that way.

Here is an example. When I was seventeen years old I was in a period of my life which involved dramatic changes. As a child, I had imaged myself as a shy wallflower. As an adolescent, I began to associate with a different group of peers and started seeing myself in a new light. At the time of completing high school, I found out that I was the valedictorian of my class. Now, in my earlier years, I would have fully expected that, having always been a straight "A" student. But in the last two years of high school I had become somewhat rebellious, had started being self destructive by taking drugs, so I was surprised that I was still at the top of my class. I attended a large school of 3000 students, so my graduating class had 750 students.

I was, therefore, faced with a dilemma. The "old" Laurel, studious, intellectual, responsible, shy, "egghead," obedient, was proud of being valedictorian and wanted to please her mother and teachers by giving a speech at graduation. The "new" rebellious Laurel, gaining approval from a destructive peer group and striving to develop independence, wanted to say "forget this establishment stuff. I won't even give a speech." The first choice of which I became aware was, "Whom do I please?" I was caught in the middle. When I gave it more serious thought, I decided that the purpose for giving a valedictory address was to offer what I knew and had learned. There was a higher purpose for giving a speech than pleasing the authority figures in my life. The purpose was for me to be influential, to perhaps change someone's life or stimulate someone to think in a new way. I knew that my experience was not unique and I wanted to offer something that could improve education for students who came after me.

There was a part of me that was intelligent enough and aware enough to realize that my rebellion was destructive. There was a part of me that knew that I had "gotten away with" settling for less than I was capable in the last two years of my high school education. I had learned how to play the game, to choose classes that were easy for me so that I could still excel academically without challenging myself to the greatest extent I could. Deep down, I was disappointed in myself for following the line of least resistance because I knew I had missed opportunities to find out just how talented and versatile I could be. I wanted to change this in myself, and I thought that by offering what I knew it would stimulate other students to change that kind of attitude before it was too late for them. I also thought I might stimulate some teacher to see how important their influence could be. None of my teachers had ever questioned my behavior, none had ever counseled me about drugs nor had any ever noticed that in the last two years I had challenged myself less than the previous years. There was a part of me that wished they had.

I decided to give the speech. I carefully formulated the main ideas I wanted to get across. I had heard other graduation speeches that were somewhat boring and I wanted this one to really *say* something. I thought about what education meant, what its value was, how it could aid students. I knew that the importance of school was for learning, and I also knew that grades were not always an evaluation of how much had been learned. Some grades were indicators of how well the students were able to please their teachers. I knew this from my own experience. I wanted to let people know that although I was valedictorian I had not lived up to my capabilities, and the grades which evaluated who was ranked at the top did not necessarily reflect the quality of the education. Admittedly the "rebellious Laurel" had a part in writing this speech. I knew that there would be some shock value in saying that grades weren't everything!

Since I completed my coursework in January and the graduation ceremony was in June, I had six months to write and practice this speech. Every day I read the speech and imagined myself giving it to a huge audience. With a graduating class of that size, the commencement ceremony was held in the football stadium. I drove by the stadium to see what it looked like and where the stage would be. As I imaged myself delivering the speech, I memorized the words and created clear thought-form images of what I wanted to say. I had included in my speech an anecdote about a math teacher who taught imitation rather than reasoning. She would teach trigonometry by giving us sample problems and categorizing the problems. Then we were to copy the way the problem was done with other similar problems. One day, an enterprising student figured out a different way to arrive at the solution. She was eager to share it with the class, but the teacher would not let her. She was afraid that Karen would confuse the class. I remember being infuriated, because I wanted to know the new way, and I could tell that the teacher was threatened by this inventive and curious student. Although I did not use the teacher's name in telling the story in the speech, I expected that this story would shock some of the audience, so I practiced telling it and pausing at the right moment for impact to hit home.

All of this practice was done mentally. I never practiced the speech out loud, but I practiced it over and over in my mind. The words became a vehicle for my expression. Rather than woodenly repeating words I'd memorized, I knew the words so that I could really tell the story I wanted to tell. I had a clear idea of the main point I wanted to make: school was for education and it was important for all of us to respect that. Students and teachers should focus on learning, and grades should be for evaluating, not for determining how much learning is taking place or the value a student has. The more I visualized myself creating this idea and giving it to the audience, the stronger it became, and the more desirous I became of giving it freely.

The day of the graduation, the stadium was filled with close to two thousand people. As I walked up to the microphone, I was filled with the immensity of the place and the desire to give and to change people's lives. I wasn't even nervous! I was excited, thrilled, and could feel the anticipation. Because I had visualized this scene over and over it seemed very familiar, like I had been there before. And I had — in my imagination! When I started speaking, I was a little startled because I had never heard my voice over a microphone before. This added to the ability to use my emotions, for in hearing my voice come over the public address system, it lent a kind of objectivity. I could hear myself as if it were another person speaking.

One of the benefits of visualizing and practicing this speech was the freedom it gave me to place all of my attention on giving to the audience. I had no attention on what they were thinking of me, how I appeared or sounded or what I looked like, whether I would "mess up." I simply gave what I wanted to give, and offered it freely. It was surprisingly easy.

This kind of visualization can work for anyone in any endeavor. Musicians use it — they practice the notes of a piece over and over and image themselves artfully playing the keys or plucking the strings. When the time comes for the performance, they need not give any attention to the mechanics of the instrument, they can express themselves through the vehicle of the instrument to play music. I know a woman who has been studying the art of karate for several years. When she practices *katas* which are a series of movements, she concentrates on her form, on using her mental and physical energy most efficiently, on the precision and grace and scientific principles with which her body functions. As she repeatedly practices these dance-like motions, she gives full attention to what she is doing. When she cannot go to the *dojo,* she practices in her mind. Riding a bus, waiting for a friend, in her spare moments, she moves through these motions in her mind. When called upon to act in self defense, or in sparring with a karate partner, she moves swiftly, surely, and exactly. Through the use of mental imagery and physical practice, she is becoming a karate expert.

It is important to know that visualization does not take the place of physical practice and preparation. You cannot give an effective speech by visualizing yourself on a stage if you have not written or prepared or researched a speech to give! This is pretending. When you pretend, you actually increase your anxiety because you are always afraid of being found out. You cannot play excellent music by picking up an instrument without studying the notes, unless you are going to improvise. Even then, you need to develop skill through practice with learning how the instrument functions.

The mental imagery directs your body's actions. The use of the visualized images gives direction to the actions you perform. In combination, you learn how to use the experiences for the expression of your Self. As adults, we usually have little awareness of the importance of using the mind to direct our actions but often when we experience a physical injury we are forced to give attention to this relationship. There was a man named Leonard who suffered severe nerve damage in a motor-cycle accident. As a result, his motor functions were impaired and he was temporarily paralyzed. Leonard was a very active person who hated being handicapped. He had goals: he wanted to teach children, to build a house, and to educate people about saving the environment from pollution. He was also very proud, and didn't like other people pitying him. He was highly motivated, and gave great attention to the physical therapy he received. For several hours a day, Leonard exercised in a whirlpool, regaining some muscle tone and re-learning how to cause his muscles to move. But the most important part of Leonard's therapy was a daily visualization in which he imaged himself walking, moving freely and easily. Leonard discovered that when he was angry at his paralysis it was fairly easy to cause some motion in his legs, because his *desire to move* was so strong! He would think, "I *will* walk! No one's going to stop me!" He would think about what he wanted to accomplish with his life and the need to have a fully functioning body for these purposes. This strong desire-thought-image propelled energy through his body. When he was tired, when he had gotten distracted from his belief in himself, Leonard would think, "Why bother? I have so far to go... what's the use?" At those times, Leonard's muscles simply didn't respond. After awhile, Leonard began to see that his *thoughts* were the most important factor in pulling energy into his body and causing it to move. This realization spurred his excitement and with practice and time, he learned to walk again.

When you visualize a new activity, it is important to believe in yourself. If you have always thought that you were not athletic, you might find yourself visualizing throwing a ball into a basketball hoop and having it bounce off the rim. Or throwing a bowling ball into the gutter, or missing the ball every time you come up to bat. In these cases, you are also using visualization! If you have not experienced success at the task you are attempting, watch those who are successful so that you can receive images in your brain of effective shooting, batting, or whatever you want to do. Then, image yourself in the place of the person who is successful. Image yourself over and over performing the action with grace, speed, expertise, or the qualities you desire. Then, in your physical practice, your actions will be directed by these productive, positive thoughts.

Using visualization you will find that you can be good at a task from the beginning. Who says you have to fall flat on your face just because you are a beginner? When you have practiced in your mind before you ever set your hand to a task, it will be familiar and easy for you to accomplish.

Relationships

In your practice of visualization, it is tempting to want to create for other people. Mothers often want to visualize their children doing well in school, lovers want to image their partners being attentive and loving, coaches want to visualize their proteges excelling in sports. But each one of us is an individual, we have own purposes for being alive, and we therefore have unique desires. We have free will and it is a choice for each of us to determine how we will create our own lives!

There are many different ways in which we associate with other people. From the earliest years of life, we learn love through relating with our parents and perhaps siblings. As we grow older, we learn how to give and receive, how to share, how to communicate, through association with family and friends. In adolescence we begin to explore the realm of romantic love and discover new forms of expression. We have co-workers, bosses, teachers, students, teammates, apprentices — many different people with whom we share ourselves, with whom we learn and grow. In all of these forms of association, we have opportunities to discover what makes us unique. Only *you* can give to the world what *you* have to offer!

We live in a world with people all around us, but many people have continual conflicts with their associates, whether they be spouse, business partner, parent, boss, offspring, or friend. I know a woman named Alice who was always complaining about someone in her environment. She was angry with her husband for his inattentiveness, annoyed with her children for their irresponsibly, irritated with her preacher for his self-righteousness, upset with the clerk at the supermarket for her slowness. She never seemed to be content with anyone, and certainly would not admit that she was causing some of these problems. Alice wanted the other people to change, convinced that if only her husband paid her more attention she would be happy, if her kids would straighten up she could be proud of them. If her preacher had a little more compassion she might listen to him and if the supermarket hired someone intelligent she would get better service. Alice was rather unpleasant to be around since she was continually finding fault with other people. One day her ten year old daughter said to her, "Mom, I love you even when you're crabby. Do you love me when I'm sloppy?" This took her by surprise, and she said, "Crabby? Me?" "Oh, yeah," the child said,"Everyone at school calls you 'the crab' but I just tell them you're moody." The child's innocence was so sincere her mother listened and started paying attention to herself. "I guess I *am* kind of irritated most of the time. I'll try to be more pleasant."

Alice imagined what it would be like to smile and enjoy her husband's company instead of barking at him. Lo and behold, she found that he gave her much more attention when she was pleasant to be around! She started to praise her children when they had done a good job, and although she continued to give them the discipline they needed, she made sure to verbalize her love for them and to give them more hugs. Alice discovered that as she practiced being more loving and compassionate she started to like people more, she was willing to listen to them and she started to develop respect for their ways of thinking and expression. In a relatively short period of time Alice changed from a negative, complaining nag to a pleasant, loving, caring person.

People oftentimes use visualization to create images of the other people they want in their lives, but the secret to creating the kind of relationships you desire is to image *yourself* as you desire to be. You cannot change another person. You can influence others, you can touch them with your love, you can give to and receive from them, you can communicate with them and create with them. But your imagination is within your own mind and creates your own self. One of the greatest joys in life is to associate with other people who are different from ourselves, for through knowing them we can learn to expand our own thinking. Each person has a different point of view, and as we listen to them we have opportunities to learn from them. As we share our thoughts with them, we can influence them and arrive at greater understanding of our own thinking. If we *did* succeed in making someone be how we wanted them to be, we would rob ourselves of the benefit of receiving what they have to offer to us.

Let us use for an example the desire for a "perfect" relationship with a member of the opposite sex. Many of us have been raised on fairy tales to believe that all we need to find is the "perfect" mate, the prince charming or lovely princess, and we will be happy and whole and complete. An idea based on Hindu mythology which has recently gained popularity is that in the beginning the soul was split in half, and each of us is a half-being wandering around looking for a mate to be our "better half" and make us whole.

These ideas are not entirely true! We are each potentially whole; what we lack is the experience and understanding of how to create. There is an ever present urge within each of us to grow, to create, to express, even to master talents and skills. Have you ever seen a plant reach toward the light? We are somewhat like that, reaching for greater awareness of our own selves. Associating with other people provides an avenue for Self expression, it gives us a place to discover more fully who we are and what we have to give. The "soulmate" that people seek is actually their own soul, the inner Self which stores the understandings we build. When we are actively creating and developing self awareness, we are "whole" and happy. Relationships of all kinds are wonderful vehicles through which we can expand our awareness of ourselves, for in giving to another individual, in receiving from another, in sharing love, we learn completely who we are and about the dynamic, creative power of love. In an intimate committed relationship with one partner we can experience the most complete expression of ourselves with another as we share mentally, emotionally, and physically.

To develop this "wholeness," decide what qualities *in you* you desire to give, to share, to explore and experience with another person. Who do *you* want to be in the relationship?

Image yourself as you desire to be, the ideal person you want to become and express. Image yourself being affectionate, warm, loving, sincere, attentive, or whatever qualities you want to develop and practice. Image yourself sharing these beautiful attributes with another person, but leave the face off the image of the other person. By imaging and practicing to become the ideal *you*, you create yourself as an attractive, magnetic center of vibrant thought. Other people will be attracted to the thought-form image you create.

How do you create a satisfying relationship without trying to mold another person in your image? The key is to first decide what your ideals are in life. If you are wanting a business partner, you must first decide what your ideals are for your business and then look for someone with compatible ideals. If you want to locate a roommate with whom you can live, determine what you desire ideally in a living situation and then find out if your prospective roommate has similar ideals. If you desire to be married, write out what you want in a marriage — friendship, sharing a home, communication, and so forth. Then you can decide if you are compatible with another person who has formulated their own ideals.

When you have determined what is most important to you in life, you can readily assess when you meet another person if the two of you have compatible ideals. For example, if you are looking for a romantic partner, you can like someone and think they are sexy and attractive, but unless you have compatible ideals it will be difficult to form a lasting, creative, satisfying association. You create your individual ideals *first,* then determine to what extent your individual ideals are compatible with another. If they match, it is probable that you can create a productive relationship. If they are widely divergent, you are setting yourself up for unhappiness. Remember this: you cannot make another *person* your goal. People move, they change, they die. When you build your life around another person you are denying your own identity. You build your life around your ideals, and then cooperate with other people in the creation of those ideals. For example, suppose that friendship is very important in your life. Communication is very important to you.

Perhaps other essential elements to your happiness are spiritual development, travel, music, and teaching. When you associate with another person who shares these ideals, you can create a dynamic life together. But suppose you meet someone who thinks that material success is most important, who likes to spend most of his time alone and prefers to keep his thoughts to himself, who does not believe in a Supreme Being, and who is a homebody who likes to stay close to the roost. As attractive as you may find this person, it is likely that in a short time you will be bored or he will try to keep you from your travels. Either one or both of you may begin to put the other one down. This is not necessary! It does not mean that one person's goals are right and another one's are wrong, it is not a case of better or worse; it is simply a matter of different choices and ideals. When you share ideals with another person, the common ideals around which you build your individual lives will form a link upon which to build a partnership.

These same principles will work for forming any kind of association. There were a couple of women who wanted to create a local organization to raise money for civic projects. Jill's idea was to create large fund-raising projects in order to support local projects like renovating buildings and beautifying the downtown area. Sally wanted a group that would share creative ideas and projects together. Her primary focus was getting to know other women in town and developing friendships; the money raised was secondary. For Jill the primary objective was to raise money and the friendship was a fringe benefit. When Jill and Sally started the women's guild they briefly discussed their ideas but did not verbalize clearly what their ideals were. Each had her own idea of what she wanted, firmly pictured in her own mind, but neither one communicated. When they initiated projects they began to run into conflicts because neither one knew what the other's priorities were. Jill would come up with projects that could raise large sums of money, like selling raffle tickets, but Sally rejected those ideas because they did not bring the women together for communication and artistic expression. Sally suggested projects like quiltmaking that would serve her purposes, but Jill vetoed them because she

didn't see how they would raise the funds she desired. Finally
the two women talked about their ideals and purposes, and in an
enlightening blend they learned how to add to their own interests
through cooperation. They decided to get together a group of
women to make a quilt, fulfilling Sally's desire, and then to raffle
the quilt to raise the money Jill wanted to give to the community.
This is an example of how to use a relationship to give as well
as receive, and how a little communication about ideals can go
a long way to resolve conflict.

Remembering that we each have free will helps us to live
the kind of life we desire and to respect the choices of others.
With the freedom to choose, we also have the responsibility to
choose wisely. We may not always agree with the choices
another person makes — we would choose differently. Understanding our differences helps us to understand our own
uniqueness and aids us in learning to love others.

It is important to know that when you are making
decisions that concern other people, you need to consider
yourself in relationship to the whole. Do the conditions and
circumstances you desire blend with the other person or people
involved, or does one person's desire override everyone else?
Cooperating with your desires and with the desires of other
people may mean that temporary conditions do not always fit
your ideal, but the long term benefits are worth the temporary
unpleasantness. Any new parent knows this! They will sacrifice
sleep and the temporary comfort of their own body to serve the
needs of their infant child who wakes up at 3:00 a.m. wanting to
be fed. The parents have a desire to give love to the child and to
satisfy his or her needs and they know that their own needs for
sleep will be met as the baby grows older. One who has imagined
themselves being the kind of parent they want to be can practice
this kind of proper perspective.

When you cooperate with another person, you learn to
consider their needs. You learn to be generous, compassionate,
respectful, and understanding. Oftentimes, idealistic people
become disappointed or bitter when they discover "faults" in
another person. But human beings are not perfect! The more
you view relationships as experiences for your own learning and

growth, the more willing you are to accept another individual's learning and growth.

For example, I know a woman named Mary who is very idealistic, strong, committed to her beliefs, goal-oriented, determined, interested in education, leadership, and creative endeavors. Through the processes described in this chapter, Mary decided what kind of romantic relationship she wanted to pursue and imagined herself expressing the qualities of love, warmth, affection, and beauty she wanted to give. She had already determined her ideals in life and created an image of sharing those ideals with a man equally committed to being a leader and educator. She wanted to be involved with a man who was self sufficient, mature, willing and desirous of learning, and creative. She broadcast her desire mentally and also communicated her desire verbally. She kept her mind alert and watched for the individual to enter her life who possessed the qualities she desired.

As expected, Mary met a man named John who was creative, assertive, a leader, with strong ideals and values, who shared a desire to be affectionate and warm and to become a close, intimate friend. Both Mary and John wrote down their ideals in life and discovered that they had compatible desires. They shared not only mental and spiritual goals, but many physical goals as well. It seemed to be a match made in heaven!

There was one major problem in the association, however. Mary discovered that John had a serious disease. The disease was one that could be controlled with proper nutrition and exercise, but it necessitated him taking daily medication and caused him to be physically weak. In all other ways Mary found John powerfully attractive, but she was afraid that John's disease would shorten his lifespan and cause a premature end to their association. Mary had a choice. She could "throw out the baby with the bathwater" and decide not to pursue a relationship with John based on her fear of his early deterioration and death. She could decide to commit herself to developing an intimate relationship with John, knowing that there was a probability of complications resulting from his disease. She could also be indecisive, giving herself to some extent to the relationship and to John, holding part of herself back for fear of being hurt and abandoned.

Mary decided that the benefits of committing herself to a relationship with John outweighed the problems. She knew that if she gave herself wholeheartedly to John, she would receive the fullness and depth of love. She also knew that there was the possibility of an early end to their association, but she decided that she would rather experience the joy and fulfillment of sharing a creative union for as long as it lasted than to cut herself off from the love because of fearing loss. People asked Mary, "Why did you choose a mate with a chronic illness?" Mary responded that she had not chosen an illness, she had chosen a creative, intelligent leader who also had an illness.

Mary was wise in recognizing that people are human; they have faults, they have places of misunderstanding along with their virtues, strengths, and understandings. When you choose to associate with another person, you receive a package deal! It is important to be aware of *what* you are choosing and to know that the productive qualities you choose, the productive elements of the association form the basis of your choice. When productive qualities outweigh the unproductive ones, you can be reasonably sure you have made a good choice. By the same token, if the detriments overshadow the benefits, you will probably want to make a different choice. If you are associating with a person who beats you, who keeps promising to change and then repeats the same destructive thinking and behavior, you are denying your own worth as an individual to subject yourself to such abuse.

One of the benefits of visualization is that you can image yourself being compassionate, understanding, honest, and helpful with another person. Rather than being annoyed or irritated or angry at another's "faults" or "weaknesses," image yourself aiding that person to change. Image yourself being a positive force for good, for productive change, and for healing. When the other person wants assistance, you can make a remarkable difference in his or her life. You will discover more of your own strength in this way and will challenge yourself to draw forth from within yourself qualities you never knew you had.

In this process you will discover a secret which will aid you in all of your visualizing work. This secret is called commitment. When you commit yourself to learning, you will always discover new facets of yourself. In relationships, you do not commit yourself to the other person, you commit yourself to the fulfillment of your ideals with that person. You commit yourself to expansion, to growth, to change, to learning. When this is a mutual commitment, both people are willing to do whatever it requires to understand, to harmonize, to add to their awareness and understanding.

This quality of commitment is one which you will use in creating any ideal in your life. When you commit yourself to the fulfillment of a desire, you do not let limitations interfere with you achieving your ideal. You use the "obstacles" as challenges, for each seeming stumbling block or difficult area gives you a place to reach within yourself for greater understanding, to build new qualities, to develop endurance, patience, to exercise a new skill. Committing yourself to learning will give you the motivation to understand the cause for "problems," difficulties, rough spots and conflicts and to cause creative change. When you respect your choices and strive to make choices that produce learning, you will more easily respect the choices of others.

We all face one such obstacle when dealing with difficult people. Undoubtedly you have had experiences with people who disagreed with you, people who you found unpleasant, who irritated you. Have you ever tried to "make" those people change? Have you left the environment in which they were because you didn't know how to get along? Or have you gritted your teeth and "tolerated" their presence? All of these coping mechanisms will work for awhile, but they do not solve the essential cause of the conflict. Here is a sure-fire way to use visualization to harmonize with your "enemies."

Start by learning to love people as companions in the universe we share. This may seem like an abstract concept, but the more you practice giving your undivided attention to the individuals you encounter, the more you practice imaging them as creative human beings, the easier it will be for you to perceive each person as a soul. When there is someone who irritates you, write their name down on the top of a sheet of paper. Then, list all the reasons why you are inharmonious with them. Do not hold back, write down the smallest to the biggest irritations. For example, they crack their gum when you are trying to work, they are noisy, they don't listen, they are inconsiderate, they are selfish, etc. List everything that bothers you about them. Then, learn to achieve harmony with that person. Ask yourself, in what way am *I* like this? This will require honesty, for it is difficult to see in yourself a quality that is unpleasant. But, when another person irritates you, it is certain that *in some way* you are like that. As a friend of mine says, "you spot it, you got it!" Once you have identified in what way *you* are like that, practice changing it *in yourself*. This is the key to harmonizing with another: you harmonize your mind to theirs, you control and understand your emotions, don't try to control the other person!

In the beginning you will find it a challenge to practice this kind of self honesty. Here is an example of how it works. There was a woman named Nancy who irritated her co-worker Sharon for the reasons listed above. They worked in an office that had little cubicles which created the illusion of privacy but which had no doors, no ceilings, and no sound insulation. Nancy used to come to Sharon's desk in the morning, plop herself down, crack her gum, and talk about her daughter, her husband, her church activities, everything except the work she or Sharon needed to do. She had little awareness that she was bothering Sharon and was inconsiderate of her needs. Sharon never said a word, she just silently fumed about it. She never asked Nancy to leave, nor did she tell her that she was trying to concentrate. Instead, while Nancy jabbered on, Sharon mentally told her to shut up, argued with her, ignored her, or blamed her for the distraction. Although outwardly pretending to be polite, in her own mind Sharon was very inconsiderate of Nancy's need to have someone listen to her. Sharon did not speak her thoughts out loud, but by being engrossed in her own thoughts she tuned Nancy out, did not listen, and was equally rude.

Although Sharon's outward expression was different from Nancy's, the very things that irritated her were the same attitudes she practiced in her own thinking. Once she identified these with by making a list she started changing them. Sharon began to listen when Nancy came over to her cubicle, giving her complete attention. Do you know what happened? Nancy became at peace with the attention she received and did not stay and talk for so long. Sharon was able to respect her and to give her the listening ear she wanted, and Nancy was then prepared to face her day and go about her work. Sharon also practiced telling Nancy when she wanted to be alone instead of berating her for being insensitive and yelling at her in her mind for not knowing what a disruption she was. Sharon had been expecting Nancy to read her mind which was irresponsible and inconsiderate, her own way of being selfish by thinking that Nancy would automatically know what she wanted.

Within a short period of time Sharon learned to reconcile her conflict with Nancy. They became good friends as Sharon understood Nancy's needs and practiced greater consideration. She learned how she could be insensitive and uncaring and though outwardly quiet, inwardly she was self-centered, consumed with her own thoughts. By identifying what she "spotted" in Nancy, Sharon could change it in herself. When you are willing to cause change in yourself, you will learn how to be a friend to anyone. Understand that this does not mean that you sacrifice your soul desires or become a doormat to another person. It means that you are willing to be responsible for causing change, for initiating communication when necessary, for resolving the conflicts that occur. This gives you a great deal of power because you always have the tools for causing change at your command.

Decision Making and Planning

Have you ever seen the cartoon of a man or woman who has painted themselves into the corner of a room? Although this is a cliche for poor planning, it also illustrates the pitfall of one who fails to visualize. In every area of life, we can be more effective and directed by visualizing the end results we want to attain.

Recently I watched a television program that featured a young woman who was afraid to take her driving test. Having failed several tests previously, she was afraid of repeating the same mistake. Her downfall was parallel parking. In the scene in which she approached the markers for the parking test, the young woman began to sweat and the terror mounted. Her instructor, a kind Oriental woman, wisely told her to visualize the car like a snake, slithering into the space. "See it slithering into the space and image yourself in control of it." Of course, the young woman followed her advice and parked the car correctly. This is an example of how visualization can be used to accomplish a task that seemed impossible. Visualizing the end results gives the mind a direction.

People often find themselves so busy running around doing activities in their lives they do not complete what they start. With many different desires, how do you determine what you can fit into a day? How do you know what you can realistically expect to accomplish, when you are wasting time and when it is well spent? How do you organize your life to include all that you desire? With visualization you can begin to plan your life much more effectively. By imagining your goals and activities, you will begin to form an idea of all that you need to complete your desired objective. You will have some idea of the length of time you need to invest to produce your desire, and will become more adept at foreseeing potential problems so that you can correct them in advance.

For example, let us say that you are going to host a dinner party but are not sure what steps to take. Sit down and imagine the night of the party. Visualize the whole scene, from beginning to end. "Zoom in" on your picture so that you can imagine every detail. This complete visualization will aid you to determine what steps to take to create the event as you desire. Who will be there? How many guests do you want to invite? This gives you an indication of how much food to prepare and how many chairs you will need. What kind of personalities do these people have? This may determine what kind of entertainment you want to provide — music for dancing, parlor games, conversation, and so forth. You may also use your imagination here to decide what kind of food you want to make — as you picture your intended guests you may remember that Mary is a vegetarian, Joe loves spicy food, Harold told you last time that your stir-fry was the best he'd ever tasted. Imagine what you want to wear, what you want to serve for drinks, what kind of decorations you will have. These factors may be related to the activities you visualize including at the party. You may decide upon an Oriental theme because of your guests' love for such food; in this case, you may visualize yourself wearing a kimono and decorating the room with fans and lanterns. Perhaps you visualize your guests eating fondue, and you know that you do not own a fondue pot. In that case, you will have to buy or borrow one. How will your guests know about the party? Imagine the time it would require to mail out invitations or to make phone calls and decide accordingly which method of communication to use. If you have children, where are they? Are you imagining them included in the party? Are your guests' children welcome? Or do you intend to include adults only? By visualizing the conditions, you will be able to determine how the quality of the party would change with or without children, and this will influence your decision. If you decide you want the party to be for adults, you will need to include finding a babysitter in your plans, or arranging for your kids to stay at someone else's house for the evening. In your image you may see your living room clean, with soft lighting and candles. But today your living room is messy and the lighting is harsh. Some of your preparation, therefore, will be cleaning the room and obtaining softer lights.

This kind of visualization improves with practice. In the beginning, you may imagine that it takes very little time to do a task, and then discover that it requires more time than you planned. The next time you are imaging a similar event you will plan more time. You will also find that the more you exercise your imagination the better you become at including details and therefore anticipating the many different elements that make up a particular project. The more completely you visualize the event as you want it to occur, the more details you will imagine and the more prepared you will be. Even if you have difficulty organizing your thoughts, you will find that the imagery will help you. By imaging what you desire, you foresee or perceive the various components of the final scene. Then you can separate out which elements need to come first, second, third, and so on. Using our party example, you may have difficulty determining what kind of food you want to serve, but after you have imaged the guests you intend to invite you can choose the most appropriate meal based on their tastes.

Creative imagery can even help you learn how to be organized. I have used imagination to set up office spaces, to organize kitchen cabinets and workplaces, to file papers and to pack suitcases. The key is to imagine *how you will use* the objects you want to put in order. For example, in arranging cabinet space, visualize what appliances and tools will be used more often. These are the ones you will want to be most easily accessible. Who will be using the space? How tall are they? You can visualize what height will be within easy range for the person to reach who will need to use it. If it is an area that will serve many people's needs, imagine who else will be there. When you put things in a particular place, will it be easy for someone else to find? Will they have to move something out of the way to see or find the item they want to use? These questions can be easily answered by imagining the scenes, who will be in them, what they will be doing, how they will be using the objects you are organizing.

When you completely picture an event in your mind, it helps you to relax. No more do you have to worry, wondering if you have everything taken care of. You will *know* what you have taken care of because you will have imagined it. When you *do* worry, it is usually because you haven't visualized the upcoming event, or your visualization has been vague. When it is vague, with little detail, oftentimes you have left out important items. You may be late for an appointment because you forgot to include in your image the time to iron your clothes, since you neglected to visualize what you were going to wear ahead of time. Therefore, when you find yourself worrying, give yourself a few moments to put all of your attention on visualizing the event from beginning to end in detail. "Look" into the picture to see the details so that you can determine what else you need to do to create the desired outcome.

Visualization may also be used for decision-making. By practicing to imagine the probable outcomes of different choices you become clairvoyant. The word "clairvoyant" is French, and means "clear seeing." When you imagine what will probably occur as a result of a particular choice, you do see clearly. Suppose you are faced with a decision that troubles you. You may have several options, and all seem feasible. What to do? Which one to make? What direction to take? Sit down, relax, and visualize step-by-step what will probably occur with each choice. Imagine not only short term future, but as far as you can image. This will aid you to determine which course of action will be most satisfying and will keep you from impulsively jumping in and out of conditions with little contentment. This use of creative imagery is especially important for "major" decisions that will have long term effects, such as marriage, career, and education.

There was a young woman named Chris who used her imagination to help her make a major life choice. As a sophomore in college she was considering transferring to another school. She had received a good education so far, but decided that she wanted to change to a larger university. Although she still had not chosen a major, she had a good idea of her interests and the subjects she wanted to pursue. After applying to several schools she narrowed her choices to two: a private university on the East Coast and a state school in the Midwest. Both were Ivy League caliber and both offered similar quality education. But there were several personal factors that entered into the decision as well. Chris was already attending college on the East Coast, had grown up in that area, and had family who lived close by. She had a boyfriend who was to be attending law school near the eastern university she was considering. The midwestern university was halfway across the country in an area in which she knew no one. Chris visited both places, and received the impression that the students at the private eastern university were somewhat snobbish. The people she met at the midwestern university were more friendly and exhibited a welcoming attitude she was not accustomed to on the East Coast. Both campuses were lovely, but something about the midwestern college struck her fancy — the area was surrounded by trees, the buildings were stately and architecturally intriguing, the extracurricular activities included many concerts, museums and cultural events. There was an excellent architecture school and law school and these were both fields Chris had considered for graduate study.

Chris made a list of pros and cons about attending each school, and found that the lists balanced each other. She then imagined herself at each school, picturing the people she had met, visualizing herself walking around, sitting in the classrooms, attending the cultural events on campus. She also imagined herself being separated from her boyfriend and family at the midwestern school. She did anticipate sadness and discomfort, but she also wisely visualized far enough into the future to imagine that she would make new friends. She figured that if her relationship with her boyfriend was solid it could survive a physical separation, and if her only reason for choosing the eastern school was to be near him, she would end up resenting him in the long run. After really getting into the spirit of each image, it became clear to Chris that she could image being happy and stimulated at the midwestern university much more readily than the eastern one. She knew that she could survive at either place and that both would offer an excellent education, but with those factors being equal the atmosphere and attitude of the midwestern school suited her temperament more. She was ready for a change, and having always lived on the East Coast she imagined the different outlook in the Midwest as very appealing. As a result, she chose the midwestern school and was very pleased with her decision. The attitudes of the people there were as she had imagined and she appreciated the change.

This kind of visualization is especially effective when there is an emotional situation that is difficult to handle. Are you considering a divorce? Imagine the probabilities of the relationship, not just tomorrow or next week, but next month, next year, for five years. Is your difficulty temporary or do you foresee it continuing and becoming worse? You can do the same in a job situation. Perhaps you are considering firing an employee whose performance is less than satisfactory but you have difficulty disrupting the status quo, particularly when it affects someone else. What is the likelihood of change? How do you imagine that this kind of thinking and behavior will be a few months from now? Visualize the events coming up, the probable outcomes, and it becomes much easier to determine what will be the most satisfying choice to make. You can also decide by doing this what kinds of changes to make *now* to change the lines of probability. For example, suppose that you are in a marriage that is not very happy. Maybe the primary difficulty is that you do not communicate well, so that there is mental and emotional distance between you and your partner. The lack of intimacy is not fulfilling, and you or your partner or both are looking for other people to satisfy your needs. Is is easy to imagine that in a short period of time such a marriage will deteriorate. You can either let this run its course, or you can do something to change the probability. Begin communicating your thoughts, perhaps obtaining counseling to help you learn how to communicate. You can take risks by being open and honest in a way you have not been before, letting down the protective walls you have built. These changes will alter the probable outcome so that you create a happy association.

As you use visualization to anticipate the future, you will want to understand that you can never know the exact outcome of an event that has not yet happened. People make choices and thereby change the course of events. Conditions and circumstances change. Life is a continual process of learning, discovery, and exploration and we would miss out on delightful surprises if we knew everything before it happened! Visualization does help you to have greater control because it increases your awareness of options. Instead of passively waiting for what will be, letting other people make decisions for you, being a victim afraid of forces beyond your control, you can hold the keys to creation in your hands. Sometimes people live in fear because they are not fully conscious of the clairvoyance they have. So they may "feel bad" or may be aware to some extent that a particular choice will result in an unproductive outcome. But they may be in the dark as to *why* they have a bad feeling. With directed visualization you can bring these fears to light. You can turn worry into planning. You can change apprehension to facing facts. "Positive thinking" does not mean that you put on blinders and pretend that everything will be fine when, in fact, there are changes that need to be made. How will you know which fork to take in the road unless you know your destination? When you visualize you can see clearly in what direction you are headed. With creative imagery you move toward your desires and can tell when you are getting distracted. You thus become the commander of your life.

Techniques

You can practice visualization every day to improve every area of your life. As you experiment with the use of your mind you will discover the methods that work best for you. Following are some exercises to apply to help you create your heart's desires.

What I Want in Life List

Decide what you want. Give this some deep consideration. What is most important to you? Include physical desires and mental or spiritual qualities. Write down, in order of importance, what you most desire in life. Describe these items in detail. Then read your list every day. As you read your list, visualize yourself having and using these objects (if they are physical) or exhibiting and expressing the qualities (if they are mental or spiritual). Create your images with love and enthusiasm. Get into the spirit of your picture.

A *What I Want in Life List* is a useful tool to help you practice proper perspective. You communicate to your Self what you want and how important each desire is in relationship to the rest. You can abbreviate this list, calling it *What I WILL.* You thereby commit yourself to the fulfillment of your desires when you write them down. As you write down each desire create and include in your image how you will use it, how you will change and who you will become in the process of accomplishing it. Then invest your time in activity which will produce the expected results. You will find that by visualizing what you want you will not need to invest as much physical activity as you would if you had given your body no mental direction. You will find moreover that instead of creating approximately what you desire or settling for less than what you want, you will be able to create exactly what you image.

One of the benefits of putting physical objects on your list is that it gives you a very direct gauge to evaluate your progress. Physical objects are easier to manifest than the mental and spiritual qualities, as the spiritual ideals require time and practice to make a permanent part of yourself. Because physical objects are tangible, you can perceive them with your physical senses, and it is therefore simple to know when you have accomplished your results. I have heard people say, "This seems kind of silly. I can just go out and buy what I want. Why do I need a *What I WILL?*" There are several reasons. First, with your *What I WILL* you create *exactly* what you want for the price you want to pay. You will find with practice that you may not even have to spend money for some of the objects on your list. When you communicate, people will give you some of your desires, or you will find them for a less expensive price than you might otherwise pay. You may discover that you can trade goods or services for the object you want to receive. Second, the purpose for living is to learn how to create. All the physical possessions in the world will not bring you happiness! Your joy comes from learning *how* to create, producing understanding within yourself of your creative nature and ability. The more you discover about your own creativity the more peace, contentment, and security you experience. Physical possessions do not last; sooner or later they deteriorate. If you build your happiness around these changeable things you will find yourself becoming depressed and disappointed. When you form your identity around what you are learning about your talents, skills, abilities and creativity, you will be fulfilled. These understandings become a permanent part of yourself; they go with you anywhere you go and you can apply them to any situation in life. This is real security, solid and dependable. Third, you build confidence as you practice fulfilling desires with your list, for you come to *know* that your thoughts are creative and powerful. No longer will you be able to convince yourself that life is a matter of chance; you will build the ability to cause what you desire *at will*.

Here are some examples showing how a *What I Want In Life List* has worked for me and others. The first item I *knew* I created from the list was a pair of shoes. I put down on the list "a pair of shoes that are very comfortable, good for walking, feel as if they are made for my feet, and cost under $10." At that time I didn't have a car and I walked to most places. I have a wide foot which is sometimes difficult to fit, so the comfort of the shoes was of primary importance. I looked in shoe stores, asked people I saw who were wearing shoes I liked where they had obtained them, I tried on several pairs. None of these activities produced the shoes I desired. Then one day I went to a special sale that was being held in an indoor stadium. Many of the stores in town had special displays at this fair. There was an athletic store that had many shoes for sale. As I looked through them, I saw that there were about twenty pairs of most styles on display. There was one pair of shoes, however, that was the only pair of its style. I tried them on, and they felt as though they were made for my feet. Unlike most new shoes that need to be broken in, these were soft and very comfortable. I walked around, and could tell that they had excellent support and would be good for walking. Then I looked at the price: $9.99. This was when I *knew* that these were the shoes I had been visualizing because they felt exactly like the shoes I had imagined when I read my list every day, and they were just under $10.00. So I bought them, because I knew they were mine. The only problem was, they were suede tennis shoes. What I wanted was something a little dressier that would be appropriate for me to wear to work. Although these shoes were marvelously comfortable and great for walking, they were too sporty for business wear. But as soon as I saw them, I realized that in all the time I was visualizing, I had never imagined what I wanted the shoes to *look* like! I had concentrated on how I wanted them to *feel,* and when I put the shoes on my feet I could tell that they *felt* like the ones I had imagined.

This experience was very productive, because it helped me to adjust my visualizations to include the use of all the senses. It wasn't until I had the actual shoes in my hands that I realized I was missing an important element — the sense of sight. Because all the other conditions matched exactly what I had imaged I knew these shoes were my creation, and I was proud of my work. It helped me to recognize how I was visualizing and what to add for even more exact results.

I have practiced using a list like this for many years. In my practices I have experimented with different methods of obtaining my desires. As you try it out, you also will discover how powerful and resourceful you can be. Remember earlier I said that you can fulfill material desires without having to spend money for them? Here are a couple of examples. Terry decided he wanted a guitar. He played the piano and loved music and knew that music could be used to bring people together. As a boy scout leader, he wanted to use music as a form of creative expression and to provide a link between parents and their children at social gatherings. Terry had found that when people got together to sing, they could transcend their differences. He traveled quite a bit and decided that a guitar was a more practical instrument than a piano which would have to stay in one place and which could not be hauled to a sing-along around a campfire.

Terry imaged himself playing the guitar, surrounded by happy families, emanating love and joy. He looked at the guitars he saw other people play, asked questions about them, bought music books and started to teach himself the guitar chords. One of his friends who was a guitar player showed him some basic fingering. Then he started talking about the guitar on his *What I WILL*. The second person with whom he spoke asked him what kind of guitar he wanted. Terry did not know much about guitars but he had formed a clear image of his purpose and described it. The friend said, "I have an extra classical guitar that is just sitting in a closet. You can have it." He brought it over the next day, a beautiful guitar in excellent condition. He had even bought new strings for it. This was a simple, easy, and inexpensive desire to fulfill!

Another example is Marie who decided she wanted a bicycle. Bicycle riding was one of her most favorite forms of exercise, and the bicycle she had owned previously she gave away when she moved across the country. She did not want to pay a lot of money for a bicycle, but she did want one to ride in beautiful Colorado, her place of residence. She wrote "a ten-speed bicycle for less than $25" on her list, and imaged herself riding in the wind and sun, enjoying the scenery and becoming physically fit. Marie talked about this desire and asked questions to find out about different kinds of bicycles to determine what would best suit her needs. She was teaching adult education classes at the time and she knew that one of her students was a bicycle enthusiast who raced bikes and belonged to a bicycle club. She was aware that he owned two bicycles which he used for different purposes. One evening he was talking about a meeting of his bicycle club, and Marie asked him if he knew anyone who wanted to sell a used bicycle for a good price. He said he didn't know, but he would ask. There was another student in the room at the time, and she asked what kind of bike Marie wanted. Marie responded, "a ten-speed for under $25." The student said, "That's so funny. I just bought my husband a new mountain bicycle for his birthday and we've been trying to figure out what to do with his old one. It's an old ten-speed but it works fine. Do you want it?" Marie asked her how much they wanted for it. She said, "oh, we'd give it to you. We were trying to find someone to give it to, but everyone we know already has a bicycle." This student brought it over the next day and Marie had her ten-speed bicycle for well under $25 — no charge at all!

Several years later, Marie moved again. Once again, when she moved she gave the ten-speed to someone else, knowing from experience that she could always re-create what she wanted. When she was settled in her new home she wanted a bicycle to ride and put it on her *What I Want In Life List*. She looked at newspaper ads, checked the bulletin boards in bicycle shops and started asking around. Mary had a new friend who was a fix-it person, who liked to tinker with mechanical things and who had picked up a couple of used bicycles to repair. Marie's friend Jody found these bikes at her apartment complex, ones tenants left as trash when they moved out. Jody fixed up one bicycle and kept it for herself. She was working on the other one which needed a major overhaul. She had no use for a second bicycle, but she enjoyed the mechanics. When Jody heard that Marie was looking for a bicycle, she asked her if she wanted the one currently being repaired. Marie said, "sure!" and when Jody was finished with her work she gave it to Marie at no cost.

People often think that the *What I Want In Life List* is magic. It does, indeed, seem like magic because the more you practice using it the more you discover how easy it is to fulfill desires. Sometimes the creation of a desire comes about from discovering a resource you never knew you had. For example, a friend of mine named Frank was planning to move from the city in which he lived to attend college. He had prepared to move, had arranged to pay for his tuition at college, was expecting his final check from his job including overtime and vacation pay, and was all set for the move. At the last minute he discovered that he had less money than he thought he would to cover his daily expenses for the coming year. Frank had some spending money, but he wanted about $300 more to cover incidental expenses and did not want to have to work more hours which would take away from his study time. He wrote down on his *What I WILL* the desire for $300 to pay for minor expenses at school. He thought about ways to earn the extra money before he moved, but he was very busy and did not think he had time to work an extra job. Frank thought about borrowing the money, but decided he did not want to add that burden to himself. He visualized having the money and using it, and then released the thought.

Frank continued preparing for his move and started to pack his belongings. As he was packing, he saw the jar of coins standing on the floor of his bedroom. He had been throwing his extra change in this jar for years, and he remembered his father telling him long ago that one day he would be glad that he had saved his change instead of wasting it. "Maybe, just maybe, this is what I've been looking for," Frank thought. He stopped packing and poured the coins out of the jar and started to count. Pennies, nickels, dimes, quarters, a few half dollars. The stacks of coins grew and Frank's excitement grew as he wrapped the coins into rolls. When he had rolled all the coins he totalled the amount, which came to $321.50! Another example of the power of visualization.

The *What I WILL* can be used to create desired conditions as well as material objects. I knew a man named Joel who had dreamed of playing professional sports from the time he was a young boy. His father loved football and they used to watch games together. He played on neighborhood teams, school teams, and was chosen to play on the college team. Once Joel became a player on the college team, he wrote down his desire to play professionally and visualized it daily. Joel carefully studied the players he admired. He practiced the attitude he saw in winners, he tried on uniforms, and imagined himself playing on the professional team. Joel made his desire well known, and many of his teammates laughed at him, telling him he was crazy to think he'd rise to such heights. But, not surprisingly to Joel, his practice and determination paid off and he was indeed chosen for the professional team he desired! When he came out onto the playing field for the first time, it seemed familiar to him, and he thought that strange...until he realized he had been imagining himself on that field for years.

When you have imagined a desire for a long time, it seems very "right" when it is fulfilled. A few years ago, I decided that I wanted to earn some extra money and I also wanted to write every day. I put both of these desires on my list. I did not set limits on how I would earn the money, I just wrote that I wanted to earn about $300 extra. I also did not define what kind of writing I wanted to do; I just decided that because I love to write I wanted to include that in my daily activities.

I met an artist who had come to the School of Metaphysics to learn about dream interpretation, since she often used images from her dreams in her paintings. We developed a friendship and found one another interesting. One day we were eating breakfast at a local cafe, and she told me that she had been considering adding verbal phrases to her line of greeting cards. Prior to this time she had been producing a line of greeting cards that featured her paintings and were blank inside. This got my attention, because I had often thought about writing greeting card verses. I love to send cards and I buy a lot of them; in my search for the appropriate card I have thought, "I could write cards like these," or "I could write better verses than these." I had even written to some greeting card companies to find out their procedures for obtaining new sayings but had not responded with any subsequent action.

I told Barbara that I would love to write some verses for her cards, and she said that she would love to see what I wrote. I asked her what she had in mind, and she said she really didn't know, that her form of expression was visual and she had difficulty putting her thoughts into words. She suggested that I look at her cards and write verses as the spirit moved me and then she would consider them. She gave me about fifteen or twenty different designs and I went home to try my hand at it. I sat down at the typewriter and reeled off thoughts that were inspired by the images on her cards. The more I wrote, the more inspired I became. I thought about particular people I love and the most heartfelt sentiments I wanted to share with them. When I finished I had written about one hundred different poetic phrases for the cards. I was happy to have written from the source of my self, but I was somewhat insecure about showing them to Barbara. I did not know if she would like them, especially because she had not given me any idea what she wanted for her cards.

When I showed Barbara what I had written, her face lit up. "This is great! This is beautiful! This is exactly what I would have wanted to say but I wouldn't have even thought of it!" She wanted to use all the verses I had written, but had only planned on putting writing inside ten of her designs. She decided to purchase twenty of the phrases, however, because she had another line of cards coming out the following season and could make use of the extra verses then. She paid me $15 apiece for the one-sentence phrases to go in her cards and bought twenty. As a result, I received a check for $300 for a couple of hours of my time spent doing what I love to do — writing from my heart. Two desires fulfilled at once with *What I WILL*.

A student of mine recently told me that she doubted the efficacy of this tool because it was hard for her to believe that she could just think of something and it would appear. I replied that it was important for her to create an image of exactly what she wanted and then to act upon it, even if the activity was simply communicating the desire to others. Linda decided she would give it a try. She listed the most significant desires first, and then was stumped for a final, material desire to put on the list. She remembered that she had recently given her daughter her VCR when the daughter moved away from home. Although Linda did not watch the VCR as much as her daughter, after she had given it away she realized there were times she would like to have one. So she decided to put a VCR as her last object on the list. She talked to her friends about it, telling them that if they ever saw a used one for a good price she would be interested in buying it.

On Friday night, Linda was at home reading a book and doing some homework assignments for her metaphysics class. There was a knock on the door, and standing there in front of her was a friend who had recently gotten married. In her arms was a VCR. Linda's friend said, "I was moving in and realized that we now have two VCR's and certainly don't need them both. I remembered you saying you were looking for one, so here, you can have this!" Linda was astounded, but a part of her was not surprised, for when she put the VCR on her list she released it and said to herself, "When I receive the VCR it will prove to me that this stuff works." She had her proof, her own experience.

A *What I Want In Life List* can be used for collective goals. It is a wonderful tool to use in a business or family, or group operation. Many marriages would grow and change and be creative if husband and wife sat down together to create a *What I WILL* for their mutual desires and family experience. When I was first opening a School of Metaphysics a number of years ago, the students created a *What I WILL* list for their metaphysical center. We had a building, students, and a few chairs. We needed everything else to furnish the place. As we are a non-profit organization and the staff is all volunteer, we often use donations to take care of our needs. The students and I created a list of priorities. One of the items on the first list was a desk. I drew a line drawing of the kind of desk we wanted, with three drawers on one side, a file drawer, very large surface area, a pull-out surface for a typewriter. We put the drawing on the wall in the place where the desk would sit when we received it. Every time anyone was in the school, they saw the drawing and imagined the desk being there. With each student's visualization the thought form grew stronger, more solid, and real. One of the students was in the process of using applied metaphysics and visualization to create a business she had dreamed about for fifteen years. In establishing her business, Lori was also furnishing an office. One day, she was talking to the office supply place on the phone and asked them if they ever donated furniture to non-profit organizations. The man on the phone said they couldn't donate anything, but he did have an old desk he would sell and deliver for twenty dollars. She said fine. Lori had never seen the desk, had no idea what it was like, but she figured that twenty dollars for a desk and delivery was worth it. The next day the store came and delivered the desk. It was heavy wood, beautifully finished oak, with a huge surface area, drawers *exactly* like the ones on the drawing on the wall, with all the features we desired. When she and I looked at the picture I had drawn and looked at the desk, we stared in amazement. The actual desk was a perfect replica of the drawing, except in reverse. The drawers I had drawn on the left side were on the right side of the desk. An example of the power of many minds working together!

The following stories illustrate how several people used their *What I Want In Life List* to fulfill a desire that many fear — finding a new job in a supposedly depressed economy. First, we hear from Lynn:

"When I moved out to Colorado from Wisconsin, my friends thought I was taking a big risk to be moving without having a job lined up, a place to move into, and knowing only one family who lived out there. I saw it as an 'adventure'! I hadn't had an adventure for so long I needed to create one and move on. So I packed up all my things in a Ryder truck, towing my car behind and left 'security' behind.

"Having been an elementary school teacher for ten years, I was still in the 'August is summer vacation' mode of thinking. I wasn't too anxious to get a job right away. Soon September came along and I began to feel the pull of the familiar educational system toward school buildings and children; I began getting my resume printed up. I applied to private schools or teaching centers that were different from the public school setting. I made out my *What I Want In Life List* and number one was a teaching job in a motivating environment, enthusiastic staff of people to work with, a place where I could be very creative, yet flexible with my teaching and hours. Teaching many ages, multi-disciplinary (all subjects), for a salary. I wanted something new and different compared to what I had come from. I could feel what it would be like.

"I sent letters to tutoring centers and schools that had programs unlike the public systems. I also read my list *daily* and September rolled on. I began to get anxious. Toward the end of September I decided to look through the yellow pages again and a school's name, Rivendell, popped out from the page. 'Using the British primary and Montessori techniques.' I had visited a school in Britain and I was curious about how this school had adopted their teachings. So I called them up and made an appointment to visit.

"When I walked into the huge 'classroom' that had five teachers and one hundred kids, a bunch of tables with chairs and a huge open 'play' area, I knew this would be different. After observing for about an hour — watching four year olds and twelve year olds side by side, working independently or in small groups, I realized that something here works! By the next hour the head teacher told me there would be a maternity leave in a couple of weeks, that they hadn't advertised yet for the position, and if I was interested they would accept my application. I did not hesitate in saying yes. I *knew* this was the place I had projected for. By the end of the week I had the job and could start right away so that Ann could teach me the ropes of her job before leaving.

"I felt as if I walked right in to the very place I projected to be working at. The secretary joked about how worried she was the job wasn't posted and filled earlier and how Terri, the head teacher, wasn't in the least concerned. Maybe she knew I'd be there even before I did!"

Here is Tina's story:

"I knew I had to find another job because savings don't last forever without cash inflow (not to mention that it is good for me to have a job to feel like a valuable human being). So I looked in the newspaper, called people, and went to interviews. But to start out with I didn't have much of a vision of the kind of job I wanted.

"Then I thought about jobs I had before and what I liked and didn't like. I know I like working with computers and I had figured out that one of the most important things to me is the work environment — good quality people to work with, enough space and light, and moderate stress level. So I wrote down these conditions and started visualizing myself going to work and being cared about and supported by the people around me, being calm and happy throughout the day and using a computer.

"I attended some workshops sponsored by the University of Missouri career center in identifying values and skills, developing interviewing skills and so forth. I'm certain I was drawn to this by my perceived need for something to help give me further impetus and clarity in the job hunting process. I had seen a poster about the workshops in a place I just went to on a whim. These workshops helped me see where my skills and interests fit into the 'world of work.'

"I also attended a creativity class at the College of Metaphysics. The teachers inspired me with talk about how the great geniuses of history achieved the things they did. And also to be actively looking throughout my days for things that I want to be part of my picture for creating the conditions I desire. After that, every interview I went to I used to identify and separate desirable from undesirable characteristics for a job. I also learned about my own self value and that I have desirable and valuable skills and abilities. My intelligence, ability to focus and pay attention to detail, my college background, my typing ability and knowledge of computers. All of these could be used to obtain and do well at a job.

"I decided I would like to work in an agency dealing with education, health, or natural resources. I had several interviews with the Division of Natural Resources and wanted to work for that agency. As time went on, I thought about all the interviews I'd had and wondered, 'Why don't I have a job yet?'

"I checked on my thoughts and attitudes and reminded myself of the purpose for getting a job — to free myself from financial worries. I made sure I was convinced that I truly desired a job and started to affirm the belief that I deserved a job and would get one. Every day I visualized receiving a call from a person offering me the job that was right for me. Just to make sure, I visualized receiving three or four job offers. I saw very clearly myself picking up the phone and conversing with this person who would offer me a job. I sent this very strongly and insistently to my subconscious and the universe using will power.

"Finally, I had done all I could do. I decided the next day I would go ahead and see if I could get assistance from the Division of Family Services. I had been holding off on doing that because I thought, 'any day now I'll get a job.' I also looked for opportunities such as living with an elderly person and taking care of them in exchange for room and board. It was at this point I finally released my desire to the universe. I thought I had done that a while back, but actually it wasn't until then that I released it. The next day I got a call from the Division of Natural Resources while I was out. The answering machine message said they wanted to talk to me about a position I had just interviewed for. The next day they called back just as I was getting ready to call them and offered me a job, which I accepted."

All of these stories are true. I could fill an entire book with "manifestation" stories from my own life and lives of people I have known who use a *What I Want In Life List.* In order to experience the wonder and splendor of creation, try it for yourself. I do urge you to put some relatively small physical items on the list (like my pair of shoes) because it will be easiest for you to believe in your ability to create these. You will therefore be calling upon the powerful drawing factor of belief or faith. You will also give yourself a very concrete way to see the results match your formulated thought, thereby gaining confidence in seeing how your thoughts cause definite physical effects.

When you use your list be sure to *communicate* your desires. As you write the desires on your list, you are communicating your desire to your own self. In order for other people to aid you to fulfill your desires (and people truly do want to help one another) you need to communicate verbally as well. Linda would never have received her VCR had she not spoken about her desire with her friends. As you say out loud the words "I want..." you will add power and substance and energy to your desired thought form. The verbal communication will help you to affirm the desirability of your ideals.

You will want to use words that describe your expectation and desire. *"When* I receive my new job, I *will* go out to lunch with you," rather than, *"If* I receive that new job I *might* go to lunch with you." The words you use will "give away" your thoughts, so practice listening to yourself when you speak. When you hear the words that come out of your mouth, become aware of the thoughts and images you hold in your mind. When they are productive and creative and positive, pat yourself on the back and continue to create that kind of thinking. When they are negative or limited or despairing, change them. The beauty of free will (which all of us possess) is that we can always cause change.

As you practice using a *What I Want In Life List* daily you will discover the power of your will and imagination. When used together, these two faculties are the magic twins of creation that you can use to create anything you desire. Following are some exercises to enhance your understanding of these valuable skills.

Exercises to Strengthen Imagination and Will

When your physical body is weak, you cannot lift much weight, run long distances, or stay healthy when viruses abound. When you exercise and eat nourishing foods, you aid your body to become strong, to build endurance and flexibility and grace. You are therefore capable of greater feats than you are with an untrained body.

Your mind is the same. When you are undisciplined, you may sometimes visualize in detail and other times have vague wishes flit across your mind. You may be able to create an image for a while, but then easily become distracted from it. You may have the best intentions in the world, but be weak in following through with directed activity. These abilities are not inborn, they are learned. Just as you can strengthen your body with exercise, you can strengthen your imagination and your will.

To build a strong imagination, practice creating images. Start with something simple that you can look at to receive through your senses the intricate detail. A flower such as a daisy is a good object with which to start. Gaze at the flower for ten minutes, taking in the color, texture, smell, noting the veins on the leaves, the variations of hue, everything. Then close your eyes and reproduce in your mind's eye the detail you have observed. When the image starts to fade, open your eyes again and look at the flower, receiving the detail through your senses. Then close your eyes, recreate the image and hold it. You are practicing forming an image in your mind and holding it. You can even practice this during leisure moments. Suppose you are waiting in line at the post office. Look at any object in the room, note the detail, close your eyes and reproduce it. Open your eyes and check to see how well you have reproduced the detail.

Another exercise you can use to practice imaging is the blackboard exercise. Sit in a relaxed position, close your eyes, and imagine that there is a blackboard in front of you. Image its size, the frame around it, a piece of chalk and an eraser. You can make this a blackboard with white chalk, or the kind of greenboard used in elementary schools with yellow chalk, or whatever you desire. It's your image! Then, imagine yourself picking up the chalk in your hand. Draw a circle on the board, hold it there for several minutes. Then, pick up the eraser in your mind's eye, erase the circle, and draw another one. This time, draw a horizontal line through the circle. Hold this for a few minutes. Erase the circle, draw another one. This time, draw a vertical line through the circle. Hold this image for a little longer than you held the last one. Pick up your eraser in your imagination, erase this circle, and draw another one. In this circle draw an X. Hold this for several minutes, longer than previously, then erase it. Experiment with drawing different patterns inside the circle. This exercise will strengthen your ability to create images and to hold them with your will.

When you are using creative imagery you want to cultivate the ability to form images that incorporate all of your senses. You can practice observation to become more familiar with your separate senses. For example, when you walk into a room, notice the different smells and where they originate. Smell the musty odor of the old books, the lemony scent of the wood polish on the bookcase, the lingering smell of Aunt

Dolores' perfume. When there are odors you cannot identify, walk around the room to discover what they are. Maybe you have never before noticed that the sandalwood beads your brother wears have a distinct, if subtle, smell. Practice exercising your sense of hearing by listening to music. Listen to an orchestra and pick out the separate instruments. See if you can follow the violin all the way through the piece, then the clarinet, then the oboe. Listen to Prokofiev's "Peter and the Wolf" and identify the different animals and story characters by the musical instruments which portray each. Strengthen your identification of taste by eating new foods and identifying the spices in them. For the sense of touch, go to a department store and luxuriate in touching the various fabrics — silks, furs, cotton, wool, synthetics. Discover how you can tell the difference among them. Then have someone place an article of clothing in your hands with your eyes closed and identify the fabric from which it is made.

To strengthen your imagination using all your senses, listen to stories on tape. Fairy tales, children's stories, and novels are all excellent. As the narrator reads the story, listen and imagine what the scene looks, sounds, smells, tastes, and feels like. This is a very enjoyable way to develop imagination! You can also practice telling stories, visualizing the scene as you describe the happenings and events.

Creative imagery involves using a strong will along with imagination. Developing a strong will means learning what your attention is and where your attention is. Concentration exercises will help you to hold your attention still. You can concentrate on the second hand of a clock as it sweeps around. Give your attention to the second hand for five minutes, five times around the clock. Any time you find yourself being distracted — by a sound outside, by the heat in the room, by a vagrant thought — gradually bring your attention back to the clock hand. Pull your attention back with your will. The more you practice this, the more quickly you will notice the distractions. You will shorten the length of time it takes you to know when your attention is off your goal, the second hand. As this becomes easier and you are able to hold your attention on the second hand for a full five minutes, increase the time to ten minutes. Hold your attention on the hand for ten minutes, or ten times around the clock. When this becomes easy, practice using the minute hand. Since the minute hand moves more slowly, this will require a greater degree of concentration. Thus, you will strengthen your will in steps.

You will want to practice concentration throughout your day as well. If you are in conversation, and notice all of a sudden that you are not listening to the person who is speaking, bring your attention back to them. When you are working on a project, put your materials away before you go on to the next project. The more defined your goals are, the simpler it is to determine when you are being distracted from them. Know what you want to give your attention to, and you will know when your attention is elsewhere. The more quickly you draw your attention back to the desired task, the more efficient you will become with your time and actions. You will become much more powerful, self directed and relaxed through the practice of concentration.

Positive Thinking

The nineteenth-century philosopher and scholar James Allen wrote a classic book on the power of thought entitled *As A Man Thinketh.* "Of all the beautiful truths pertaining to the soul which have been restored and brought to light in this age," he wrote, "none is more gladdening or fruitful of divine promise and confidence as this — that man is the master of thought, the molder of character, and the maker and shaper of condition, environment, and destiny... All that a man achieves and all that he fails to achieve is the result of his own thoughts." Allen's statement illustrates a universal law of creation called the Law of Cause and Effect. Simply stated, this law is "Thought is cause, and effect is its manifest likeness."

With this in mind, can you see the importance of creating purposely cultivated positive thoughts? When life is beautiful and things are going your way, do you respect and appreciate it, or do you think compulsively, "This can't last"? When you are happy in a good relationship, do you create ways to become more loving and attentive, or do you worry, "This is too good to be true"? When a "disaster" occurs, such as having your car break down a week before payday, do you approach the situation with creative thinking, looking for your resources and examining all alternatives, or do you wallow in self pity, thinking, "This *always* happens to me"? The choice is yours to create a healthy, productive, positive life or to create one of limitation, victimization, and fear.

Many people have difficulty believing that their thoughts have the power to control inanimate objects or external circumstances. You may have kept yourself from fulfilling a desire because you encountered what you thought were "circumstances beyond your control." Any circumstance in your life is yours, and the more you learn about the mechanics of creative imagery, the more control you will have in any situation. This begins to make sense when you consider how mutable the physical world is. The nature of physical existence is *change*. Every form of physical life is in motion and therefore in the process of decay. The mountain is little by little wearing away, the chair you are sitting in is in a process of deterioration, the weather changes daily, every cell in your body regenerates every seven years. Because the physical world is so transitory, we can easily mold it and shape it with our thoughts and actions.

It is relatively simple to change conditions and circumstances in our lives once we accept and use the creative power of thought. The beauty of visualization is that it enables us to "see" beyond the present; it gives us the power to determine the course of our life. When conditions seem dismal, we can imagine something better, and that is the first step to having it! For example, suppose you are working in a dead-end job that doesn't provide you with enough money for your needs and which involves routine tasks that do not challenge you to use your highest skills. You can sit there and complain, you can wear yourself out with negative thoughts about the boring job, the long hours, the low pay, or you can imagine something different. What would you prefer to be doing? Imagine the skills you would like to be using. Image yourself in a different, more challenging position. Cause your image to be complete, including the understandings and talents you will draw forth from within yourself. Now, imagine yourself in the position you currently have, using it more fully. How can you give more of yourself than you have been giving? How can you give your attention more fully to the "mundane" tasks that face you? Imagine "going the extra mile" rather than doing just enough to get by. As you learn to appreciate your present situation you will discover the secret to abundance. The more fully you give yourself to what you have *now,* the more you will receive from your present conditions, and the wealthier you will become spiritually.

By imagining beyond your current conditions, you are causing evolution to occur. The next step is to begin looking for the kind of position you desire (remember, while you are giving yourself fully to the one you have). You have already been introduced to the methods of creating a clear thought-form image. Use these methods to image the desired condition you want. By imaging more than what you have, by seeing beyond the physical conditions that face you, you will cause change. I have heard people say, "I can't imagine that because I've never experienced it." This is a misunderstanding of the power of imagination. We are endowed with a great gift of imagination which enables us to create something above and beyond what we have experienced. Animals function from memory, or past experience. Man, the thinker or reasoner, can imagine a higher and more elevated existence than what he has already experienced. The light bulb, automobile, and computer were all invented by people who thought to themselves, "What if..." The desire to improve and enhance life fuels our creative imagination.

If you have difficulty with this, draw upon memory images and put them together in a new way. For example, suppose you have an ideal to be a teacher and you want to teach one hundred people in a class, but all you have experienced is teaching a class of twenty. All you need to do is to draw upon the images you have stored in your memory of teaching classes of twenty people and put them together. Combine five memory-images of classes of twenty students, put each class in your imagination in the same room, and voila! you have imagined a class of one hundred. Another way to do this is to draw from your memory the image of the class of twenty people, see them in your mind in one classroom, and then image each person "cloning" into five people. Each of the twenty students multiplies by five. Once again, you have imagined what one hundred people in a room would look like and feel like. One image I like to use in combining memory images together is to imagine the people "beaming up," as in the Star Trek show, being transported from whatever situation I have experienced, and "beaming down" into the new situation I am imagining. You can use whatever images work for you. Experiment and you will find the methods that are easiest for you. Visualization is fun; it can be a great joy to experiment with the many different ways to create the thoughts and experiences you desire.

In addition to using visualization for creating new, changed conditions in your life, you can also visualize particular attitudes you want to have. Your attitude is how you look at life. When you think thoughts like "I am unlucky, disasters always happen to me", you have created a victim consciousness which will manifest as disasters in your life. You can just as easily (in fact, *more* easily) create a positive attitude about life: "I have the ability to create what I want. I am a valuable being and the power to create is in my hands. I am learning how to be a better creator every day." It is easier to think positive thoughts than negative thoughts, because the natural motion of the mind is a forward, productive, creative urge. Therefore, when you create positive thoughts you are harmonizing with your mind. You have more energy. Negative thinking fights with the natural motion of your mind, and it causes fatigue. When you decide what you want and create the "how-to" attitude, that is, when you think in terms of how to create your desire, you will be flooded with energy and inspiration!

For example, a child who is eagerly anticipating Christmas will stay up late, and still jump out of bed early in the morning, animated with excitement. Even though the child may have only slept a few hours, his or her passionate desire fuels the body with limitless energy. On the other hand, an adult who hates their job may go to bed early but find themselves exhausted in the morning when they need to arise. The body has had plenty of sleep, but the dread and lack of enthusiasm drains their physical system, leaving them fatigued. When a person has something positive to expect, their mind and body prepare for the best with zest and vigor. Similarly, a person who wants to avoid an unpleasant experience will withdraw life force from their body and become tired.

If you have practiced negative thinking for a long time, it will require practice to learn to think in positive ways. With a little bit of practice you will reap tremendous results. A good way to practice creating a positive attitude is to listen to the words you say. Listen particularly for the word "if". Do you say, "*If* I get this job I will be happy"? Or do you say, "*When* I get this job I will be happy". Do you say, "I wonder *if* I will find the right dress for the wedding"? Or do you say, "I am looking forward to *when* I find exactly the dress I want"! In small or large creations, the power of your expectation is crucial. Change the "if" to "when". This will create a different attitude, one of positive expectation, one which indicates that *you* are the commander and ruler of your thoughts and your life. Listen also for words like "can't," "I don't know," "maybe," "I'll see." These words indicate doubt and indecision. Every thought you think is like a seed that you plant in the fertile soil of your own mind. When you plant seed-thoughts of doubt and indecision, you reap like manifestations. Plant seed thoughts of security, authority, and definition! Say, and think, "I will," "I know" or "I will find out," or "I will commit myself to it," "I'll plan on it."

You may already be doubting your ability to commit yourself to a project or goal which has not yet manifested. I know a woman who is afraid to commit herself to anything that she has not previously experienced, because she doubts the power of her imagination. Recently, this woman Lisa was talking about her desire to be married. Lisa's previous marriage ended in a divorce which left her somewhat cynical about relationships with men. Lisa is still afraid that if she marries she will find herself trapped into an unpleasant liaison, so she tends to avoid approaching relationships. I asked Lisa what kind of marriage she wants, and her response was, "Oh, there's no such thing as a good marriage. Men are all alike." Lisa's negative expectation keeps her from experiencing anything different! Joyce, on the other hand, has also been divorced and wants to be married. When Joyce's marriage ended, she examined in what ways she had failed to be the kind of wife she wanted to be and in what ways the relationship was unsatisfying. Then she started asking herself, "*What if* I had said this instead of ignoring the problem?" "*What if* I had gotten the job I wanted rather than thinking it would interfere with being a mother?" "*What if* I had been more affectionate?" "*What if* I had voiced my desires instead of denying their importance?" With each question, Joyce imagined a different expression and different relationship. She began to perceive how she could use a commitment with a mate in a more productive way. When Joyce met a man who seemed like a potential husband, she was scared at first that the relationship might turn sour. But she practiced the *what if*'s that she had imaged and started to see that she could be different and a relationship could be different from her "failed" marriage. Then Joyce found a ring that she started to wear on the ring finger of her left hand. She imagined what it would be like if she were married to Joe, her new beau. When problems arose in their association, instead of dropping the relationship she asked herself, "*What if* we were married, how would we handle this?" Over time, Joyce discovered that she could commit herself to change and to causing the kind of union she desired. Wearing the ring was a physical prop that helped her to imagine herself happily married. When she and Joe finally decided to tie the knot, they were on their way to a fulfilling marriage, for which they had prepared using creative imagery.

Realize that you have imagination and will to use as very powerful tools to create anything you desire. To commit yourself to a goal or project means that you imagine the completed results, and you exercise your will. The will is your ability to choose. Every time you choose to move your mind and body in the direction of your ideals, you are practicing will power. The power is in your attitude. Do you have a "can-do" attitude? Are you thinking, "I will do it no matter what" or "I've never done this before, but I can figure it out"? Then you are practicing making choices that will produce the success you desire. When you think, "I don't know if I can do it, because I've never done it before" you are thinking that you are no better than an animal, that all you can rely upon is your memory. You do have the ability and tools to go beyond your previous experience — all it requires is you *imagining* yourself being what you want and having what you want, and then moving in that direction with your choices and actions. By imagining the end results you desire, you can anticipate the activity which will produce your desired outcome. With a vague or fuzzy image of the end result, you may not know which direction to turn or what action to take. For example, let's say you want to go from Missouri to New York but you have never been there before. If you hop in your car with a vague idea of going east, you may arrive somewhere in the vicinity but most likely you will get lost! Now, suppose you look at a map and image precisely where you want go. You can observe the various routes which lead to your destination, and choose the ones which best suit your purpose — the most direct and shortest highways, the scenic roads that will take you past lakes or mountains, the routes that go by cities where relatives live who you want to visit. With a clear image in mind, you are better able to choose.

If you have trouble making decisions, if you don't know if you can do something you've never tried before, the solution is to strengthen the thought-form images you create. Visualization is your tool for causing yourself to be who you want to be and to have what you want to have. Your actions will produce the changes you desire when you are directing the physical activity with the thoughts you create. Thought directed with intelligence is the greatest power in the universe. With intelligently directed thought, you draw upon universal laws of creation. When you do not change your thought images and "try" to act in new ways, you find yourself forcing activity that results in fatigue, depression, and eventually giving up. Why go out and look for a new job when you are imaging yourself being rejected by every employer you talk to? Why spend your energy cleaning the house when you are visualizing the dirt and grime rather than the improved, clean condition? View your time as an investment, and make wise investments by putting forth activity toward a desired result which you have visualized. When you are "trying" to make a change, in most cases, you are visualizing a point at which you will fail! Why waste your time and energy for failure? Learn to expect to succeed by creating the image of the desired change, and view the choices and actions you make in that direction as an investment of time and energy which will pay off in the benefits you want.

Visualization will aid you in conquering the old, negative ways of thinking you have had in the past. Most of us have been taught in some ways that we should fear new experiences. Watch parents and how they teach this to their children: when the child is climbing on the back of a sofa, the parent says, "Don't! You'll get hurt!" As adults, often we have forgotten the messages our parents taught us, but our fears surface in subtle ways when we are approaching experiences that are unfamiliar or uncomfortable. Very often, people who want to change will try to "overcome" a fear. The image that accompanies "overcoming fear" is like having a huge boulder (the fear) that is in your way and you try to shove it aside, or climb over it, or get around it. Or perhaps the fear is like a stone wall that is blocking your path and you try to blast it with dynamite. Whatever image you have, "overcoming fear" carries with it the connotation of hard work.

There is an easier way, one which is pleasant and exciting. Forget about overcoming your fears! It is okay if you have fears; they are not your enemies and you need not demolish them or blast them to smithereens. Learn instead to cultivate the attitude of *curiosity*. Curiosity will conquer more fears than bravery ever did! Think about this: it is late at night, the room is dark, the closet door is open a crack, and some strange noise is coming from the closet. Alone, in the dark, you are afraid because you do not know what is causing the noise. You can "try" to be brave and overcome your fear to see what's there, but, trembling and frightened, you will have to force yourself to get out of bed. Now, suppose you are *curious* to find out what is making the noise. You don't even think about fear, because your drive to discover, to explore, to investigate takes the upper hand. You easily go over to the closet and open the door because you are curious to find out what is going on! This same action will work for any fear you have. Suppose you are shy, and afraid to talk to people you don't know. Quit trying to "overcome" your shyness! Practice instead being curious about the new people you can meet, to discover the interesting individuals you can encounter. Learn how to be intrigued by the new ideas and experiences you hear about in a conversation with a "stranger". You will find it far easier to be curious and interested in other people than to focus attention on yourself and your insecurities as you force yourself to "overcome" what you see as a disability.

Positive thinking can be applied to any situation which you fear. Many people ask me how to "protect" themselves from evil influence. They fear the negative influence of people with whom they work, of dark forces, of "bad vibes" in a community, of a former spouse who is bothering them. You do not need to protect yourself from anyone or anything when you develop inner strength and awareness. When you are creating strong, clear, positive thought-form images and practicing love, you are a very powerful, dynamic force. Negative thoughts will not penetrate the aura of your love and light. You do not even need to think of this as a "shield" or protective barrier, for you do not want to shut yourself off from people. Think of love and light, or awareness, as having a healing, harmonizing influence. Positive thoughts are always stronger than negative thoughts. Thinking positive thoughts will center you so that you do not even need to be concerned about the negative thoughts of people around you.

I used to work in an office of twelve people. When I started working there, I noted how negative the other people's thoughts were. It was a popular topic of conversation to complain — about the boss, the weather, the long hours, the world situation, the company, their teenagers, anything! I noticed that oftentimes one person would start to grumble, then another would jump on the bandwagon and complain about something else, then another would chime in — getting involved in these gripe sessions was a way to be popular and "one of the crowd." I decided to try an experiment. Instead of preaching about positive thinking, I would go into the office in the morning and smile and say something pleasant. When another person started complaining, I would project love to them and say a kind word. Then I simply gave it no further attention. Gradually, as I practiced saying positive statements and thinking loving thoughts, one of my co-workers noticed. She started telling me how much she enjoyed having me work there because I was always so "serene and calm," I was always so positive. She started complaining less often, and over a period of time even began to speak of the good things that were occurring in the office. Then another person started speaking in more compli- mentary ways. One by one the people in the office were influenced by my positive thoughts and statements and in a period of a few months the whole atmosphere and vibration of the office had changed. Although complaints were not completely eliminated, they were dramatically reduced. This showed me how much influence one person can have, and how strong a positive way of thinking can be.

Affirmations I

As you learn to build confidence in your ability to create, you may encounter doubts and temporary setbacks. Perhaps you are imaging yourself working as a sales representative for a particular company, you interview for the job and believe you are going to attain it, but then you find out that they have hired someone else instead. Don't lose hope! It is likely that there is a better job waiting for you...all you need to do is find it. To keep you going, to help you build a strong faith in yourself and your creative power, you may find it beneficial to use simple affirmations. An affirmation is a positive, clear statement of your desire. Just as a road sign along the highway helps you stay on the correct path, a written or spoken affirmation will aid you to keep thinking in positive ways.

When you affirm something you make it firm, you declare definitively that you are dedicated to the fulfillment of your desire. The more clearly and the more often you affirm your objective, the more solidly it becomes fixed in your own thinking. If you find yourself becoming swayed by the negative thinking of other people around you, silently chant a positive affirmation of your desire. Soon you will find that your own resolve is not so easily disturbed.

The most effective affirmations are those which have meaning for you. If you use someone else's words, be sure that those words describe an image that lives in your own mind. Or you may use another person's words as a springboard to write words that verbalize your own image in a more personal way. The affirmations you use will change according to your desires. For example, if you are visualizing yourself healing a broken leg, you might affirm, "I am healthy and full of vigor with strong muscles and solid bones." After the injury is healed you may choose to voice a completely different affirmation for a new desire.

Following are some affirmations you can use to get you started believing in yourself as a creative, mighty, resourceful, happy being. As you practice affirming your desires, you will discover words that empower you when you speak or write them.

I am happy, creative, and fulfilled.

Life is full of unlimited resources.

Wherever I am, good things happen.

I am full of joy.

I give thanks for the treasures in my life.

It is a wonderful day!

I love my life.

I give thanks for abundance and prosperity.

I look for the gift in every experience.

I am ready and willing to receive life's abundance.

I love the divinity in each person I meet.

I salute the divinity within you.

I improve the earth plane wherever I go.

I am a fountain of joy.

I give ever-increasing riches from the source of my abundance.

I am a spark of light.

I am loving and generous.

I am a positive influence on everything and everyone around me.

I bring light to every situation.

Every person I meet has a gift to offer.

I have integrity, dignity, and strength.

I am a creative, interesting person.

I am secure and at peace.

I love and am loved.

Today is full of hope.

I am intelligent and creative.

I am strong mentally and physically.

I love the people around me.

I am confident and at ease in all situations.

Every situation brings me opportunities
> *to discover more of my power, creativity, skill,*
> *and talent.*

There are sources of support around and within me.

All things are possible.

PART II

Your Inner Resources

Structure of Mind

The successful businessman and author Napoleon Hill *(Think and Grow Rich)* said, "Whatever you can conceive and believe, you can achieve." He knew a fundamental truth: your mind responds to your intelligent direction. Anything that you can imagine you can have! Throughout history, people of genius, great inventors, pioneers, winners in all walks of life have drawn upon universal principles. These principles will always work, no matter who uses them. As you practice using creative imagery you will find that seemingly miraculous events will happen to you. In time, you will know that it is not mere coincidence, that you do create situations, circumstances, and events through visualization. Visualization seems magical and mysterious when you experience its effects. To fully appreciate its magic, however, you can learn *how* it works, to wield its power at will. Then you will rank with the successful people through the ages who knew the secrets of creative imagery.

You have probably heard of the power of the subconscious mind. I have read many books that speak of its power, and have encountered popular misconceptions. One of these is the erroneous belief that somewhere hidden in the subconscious are secret desires. I have heard people who were disappointed when they did not achieve a goal and blame it on their subconscious mind by saying, "My subconscious must not have wanted me to have it" or "I must have subconsciously blocked it." This is a fallacy because our subconscious mind is designed to work for, not against us.

In this chapter I will explore the structure and function of the mind so that you have a foundation to understand how visualization works. Because there are many different ways in which people understand the mind and its functions, there are also many different names given to explain these. I am using the word *mind* to refer to a vehicle used by man the thinker. (The word *man* here comes from the Sanskrit *manu,* which means *thinker.*) The psychologist Carl Jung used the word *psyche* to describe the mind. Each of us is, in essence, a spark of light or awareness. We are individual beings, with intelligence, free will, and the ability to create. We have unlimited potential which we develop according to the choices we make. This physical world in which we live is like a vast schoolroom we inhabit to learn, to grow, and to mature.

When a child is born, he or she is a complete and whole entity with a tiny physical body. Many adults love to look at and touch little babies, because they are so perfect, a miniature expression of humanity. When a baby looks at his or her parents, he is stimulated with a desire, "I want to be like you!" We can observe children imitating their parents, wearing Dad's shoes, putting on Mom's makeup, playing house or school. A child's urge is to mature, to express, to change, and grow to be like their parents. A little child desires to be like Mommy or Daddy but has no experience, and the process of growing up is one of maturing in experience to learn how to become like the parent. It starts with the simplest acts, like pulling themselves up on a table to be able to stand.

As we mature in our physical growth, we change and develop in awareness with every experience. We live to learn how to create, to become better skilled, to develop qualities of love, understanding, wisdom, and so forth. Most of us do not remember how we started learning as babies, but we can remember learning as we grow older. I knew a woman who re-awakened a memory of learning about herself as an individual in the process of retraining herself to move her muscles. Jill had become paralyzed through an accident which bruised her spinal cord. When I met her, she was in a wheelchair, unable to move her arms or legs. She had practiced thinking and saying, "I can't" in response to any desire to use her body, and depended upon her mother to feed her, clothe her, and bathe her even though she was fifteen years old. Eventually Jill grew tired of being captive. She watched other young adults running around enjoying themselves and became jealous. Although she still enjoyed her mother's attention and nurturing, she started formulating a desire to be independent and to feed and dress herself. Jill was under a doctor's care and also visited a physical therapist regularly, but her greatest handicap was her own self-defeating attitude. One day as she was "trying" to move her hands with an exercise recommended by her physical therapist, Jill got angry and shouted, "I am sick and tired of being crippled. I want to move my fingers!" Immediately Jill felt a tingle in her hands and was able to move her fingers. Even though at first it was a slight twitch, this was a great improvement over her previous progress. She was overjoyed. Jill tried again, and was flooded with a brief memory of herself as a toddler, being fed by her mother, thinking, "I can do it myself," and batting the spoon out of her mother's hand. This experience helped Jill to remember how she had first asserted her independence. From that day on, Jill purposely formulated an image of herself as a strong, independent person, able to take care of herself and to move gracefully and powerfully. The change did not take place overnight, but with continued practice Jill learned to move her body and take care of her own needs.

This story illustrates how the thought of "I can" or "I will" or "I want" directs our physical body to operate. The reason we have a physical body is for the purpose of our learning, for we learn through experience and the body provides a vehicle for these experiences. Imagine trying to get from Los Angeles to New York without a car, plane, or train or some other vehicle. This is what it would be like to try to live and learn without a body for conveying our soul and mind!

The mind is a kind of vehicle just as the physical body is. It provides a structure which is illustrated in the accompanying diagram. The mind is not a physical "thing," so this diagram will show you how the different divisions and levels of mind interact and are structured, but it is not a picture of the mind itself. The top of the triangle is like innermost part of the self. You have probably considered that there is more to you than meets the eye. Perhaps you have even thought that there is hidden power and wisdom within you. This is true! The process of self discovery is like peeling away layers of an onion — the outer core is the toughest and as you approach the center it becomes sweeter and sweeter. Similarly, as you become more aware of your own center, you discover beauty and awareness. At the top of the triangle is Light, because at the very center of your being is light or awareness. Human beings are a unique species, with self awareness. Below Light is "I am." This is our individuality. Each individual has awareness of Self as separate from every other individual and at the same time we are all related to one another as members of humanity.

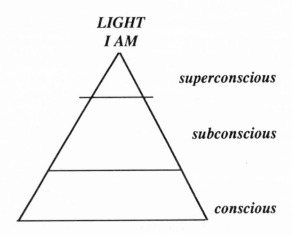

How often do we ask ourselves, "Who am I?" Everyone strives to fashion an identity for themselves and to understand who they are. The inner urge to create fuels our desire to identify who we are and how we are unique. This is easy to spot in teenagers, who often go to extreme lengths to prove to themselves that they are separate from their parents and are unique. They may grow their hair long, shave their heads, wear outlandish clothes, use slang words, all in an effort to proclaim, "This is who I am!" Adults may use other methods, more or less sophisticated, to demonstrate their individuality. John Smith may buy the latest updated sound equipment or the flashiest car. Mary Smith may put on the most inventive dinner parties. Any of these activities are attempts to discover who we are.

The mind is designed for the purpose of providing a structure which we can use to create and to know ourselves. Every time we create we develop more awareness of our unique character. The more conscious we become of the process of our creativity, the more quickly we discover who we are. The mind is divided into three major divisions: superconscious mind, subconscious mind, and conscious mind. The superconscious mind, the innermost division, is the inner divinity within each one of us. The superconscious mind contains a seed idea or plan or blueprint for our completeness as an individual. The superconscious mind is like a spark of life supplying energy to the rest of the mind.

The conscious and subconscious minds work together as a unit. The conscious mind is the division with which we are the most familiar. It works with the brain and the five physical senses. Here is where we imagine, use memory, make decisions, speak verbal language, and exercise will. Do you remember the children's story *The Little Engine That Could*? The little engine that chanted "I wish I could" over and over was able to move for a while, but then slowed down to a stop. The engine that made it to the destination was the one who chanted "I think I can, I think I can" until he succeeded. When we "wish" for success or "try hard," we create self-defeating thoughts in our conscious mind. When we think, "I know I can have this and I am willing to invest my time and energy in its fulfillment" we are creating powerful, determined thoughts in our conscious mind. The duty of the conscious mind is to create experiences in the physical world and to produce understandings. When we want to change, to expand, to become better skilled or more self aware, it starts with the conscious mind. An "understanding" is a quality or awareness of universal truth that aids us in knowing how to create. Every thought we form in the conscious mind is like a seed which we plant in the fertile soil of the subconscious mind, where it can grow to fruition. With practice, the conscious mind makes understandings a permanent part of the Self.

The subconscious mind is the division of mind which stores permanent understandings and from which intuitive faculties arise. When we have a twinge of "conscience," when something "feels" right or when we experience a mental "click" in telepathy or knowing clairvoyantly what will occur, this comes from the subconscious mind. The subconscious mind has the function of reproducing anything we imagine in the conscious mind. When people speak of the power of the subconscious mind, they are referring to this power to reproduce. Suppose, for example, you decide you want to become an accomplished speaker. This thought-desire is formed in your conscious mind. You image yourself speaking confidently and with charisma, concentrating on the new you. As you visualize this desire, you are planting a seed in your subconscious mind. The more attention you give to your desire-thought, the more you practice being the confident speaker you want to be, the more your desire will thrive. The subconscious mind nourishes your image and stores the understandings of confidence and charisma you are developing.

To live a productive, creative life means using the whole mind as a creative unit. At this stage in the evolution of mankind, many people develop an awareness of the superconscious mind through the practice or study of religion. The ideas we form and practice about God inspire us to reach for the highest within ourselves. Even people who do not believe in a God usually have an idea of some force or power greater than themselves. Most people have some concept of a great power that is benevolent, sure, omnipotent, and omniscient. They may refer to this as "God" or as a higher power or the High Self or as a "force." They may interpret it as an ultimate order, or as universal good or "righteousness" that enables people to live harmoniously. Oftentimes the moral standards people design revolve around their understanding of and desire to live up to this higher power. In any case, whatever degree of awareness and understanding we have gives us an image to which we can reach, an ideal toward which we aspire. When a person believes that he or she has a mission or important work to do in life, this is an awareness of their spiritual assignment, the "plan" contained within their superconscious mind. This is not to say that we have a pre-ordained destiny or that some higher power has laid out for us a step-by-step agenda. This is more like a seed or blueprint. It is in the conscious mind that we choose *how* and *in what manner* we will fulfill this spiritual design.

When we have some awareness of the inner urge to become our best Self, it is the task of the conscious mind to choose how to bring this about. There is a formula that is guaranteed to work to enable us to use the conscious mind in this manner. This formula for success is called *Ideal, Purpose, and Activity.* Mastering *Ideal, Purpose, and Activity* will give you the key to understanding self motivation, to providing direction in your life, to building confidence, security, and identity. *Ideal, Purpose, and Activity* will enable you to produce the things and conditions and circumstances you desire as well as offering the secrets to creating the identity and self you crave.

An *Ideal* gives you direction. It is an image of what you desire. Ideals are created in the conscious mind, through the process of forming goals. Ideals may be physical, for example, the ideal car you desire may be a red Mercury Sable station wagon equipped with AM-FM radio and cassette player, air conditioning, red leather interior, electronic windows and mirrors and seats and rear windshield wipers. The physical ideals you create are the objects you desire to have in your life. Physical ideals may also be conditions such as health, including a healthy body, with toned and flexible muscles. Ideals may be mental or spiritual qualities you want to develop in yourself, such as self expression, compassion, gentleness, discipline, confidence, and so forth. Your ideals may take the form of goals you want to accomplish such as graduation from school with a particular grade point average, or career objectives. Simply put, the ideal is what you want or your desire stated and imaged in its ideal form.

Purpose is why you want the ideal, what you will do with it and how you will use it. Purpose amounts to *who you will become* in the process of accomplishing the ideal. For example, the purpose for the physical ideal of a car may be responsibility and the accompanying freedom; that is, with your own car to drive you can be responsible for going where you want to go with the freedom to travel when you want to go there. The purpose for the healthy body may be that you want to be more energetic to serve people in your career to a greater extent. The purpose for building the mental qualities and spiritual ideals may be so that you can be a better teacher, so that you will be a good friend or an attentive spouse. Purpose can be simply described as building character.

When you fulfill a desire and then feel somewhat empty, it is because you are lacking purpose. For example, consider Aleta's story. Aleta wanted very much to be involved in a relationship with a man because she was lonely. She formed an ideal of the perfect companion, a man who would be kind and tender and gentle and supportive. Aleta met Jason, a man who was in many ways like the ideal man she had imagined. Once Aleta and Jason became involved, Aleta started to withdraw and to close herself off from Jason. She was afraid of being left alone and therefore would not allow herself to become intimate with Jason. Jason tried to win Aleta's affection, but after awhile he assumed that Aleta was not interested in him because of her aloofness, so he broke off the relationship. Aleta, heartbroken, sobbed because, as she had feared, she was alone once again. Although Aleta said she wanted a relationship, she never formulated a purpose for herself. She needed to learn how to be more affectionate, more open and trusting, but she never admitted this to herself and therefore never determined that she would practice building these qualities in a relationship with a man. Had she affirmed this purpose for the relationship, Aleta could have learned how to be different with Jason than she had with other men, causing evolution in her self. Instead, she repeated the same limiting thinking and behavior she had in the past, perpetuating the same "void" or need for learning, known as karma. If you find yourself thinking, "Why does this always happen to me?" look to see what you can learn from a situation and how you can cause change in yourself. Then you can be more purposeful in the ideals you create.

Once you have established an ideal and purpose, there is a third step which will ensure the fulfillment of your desire. This is *Activity*. Activity is what you will do to accomplish your ideal, both mentally and physically. When you have an ideal (what you want) and know your purpose (why you want it and who you will become in the process of creating your ideal), activity is the means by which you will accomplish your ideal and purpose, the "how-to." In the previous example, although Aleta was missing purpose, she did form a clear ideal and acted on it. Once she decided what kind of man she wanted to meet, Aleta frequented museums, concerts and jazz clubs — places she enjoyed. She assumed that anyone who attended these places would have interests similar to hers, and as she expected, she met Jason at one of the museums she visited. Her mental activity consisted of reasoning where she would go in an effort to meet a man of like mind; the physical activity was attending the events and initiating a conversation with Jason who was viewing a painting in the museum.

The formula for success encapsulates principles of creative visualization that have been used by successful people throughout the world. Everyone has a mind and all minds work alike. There are universal principles that operate anywhere, any time, for anyone. When you read success stories from different people in different cultures in different fields of endeavor, you can begin to see this universality. People say the same things in different words. For example: Henry Ward Beecher (1887): "It is not the going out of port, but the coming in, that determines the success of a voyage." The Bible (Matthew 7:20): "By their fruits ye shall know them." Ralph Waldo Emerson (1836); "The house praises the carpenter." Italian Proverb: "It is not enough to aim, you must hit." Herbert J. Taylor: "A good example is the best sermon."

Knowing the mechanics of visualization, how the process occurs and how to command universal principles and universal laws, you will have control of yourself and your life. Essential to the understanding of visualization is the universal Law of Cause and Effect. This law states that "thought is cause, and effect is its manifest likeness." You may have heard this as, "You are as you think you are." Everything in our universe, from the book you are holding in your hand to the chair on which you are sitting to the physical body you inhabit, was created with thought. Every inventor, scientist, artist or musician has experienced this fact. Before an artist puts paintbrush to canvas he creates an image in his mind of the scene he wants to portray. An inventor has an idea he wants to execute. Even simple tasks demonstrate the creative power of thought: the thought, "I'm hungry" precedes the thought, "What do I want?" which is followed by imagining a delicious steak, before any action is taken to cook the meal. Because this is such a natural and universal process, often we are unaware of it.

Practicing concentration exercises is an excellent way to strengthen your awareness of the power of thought. When you are a quick thinker, and you easily jump from one idea to another, it is common to have little awareness of your own thoughts. No wonder it can be difficult to believe that your thoughts have the power to create! But the person who can concentrate intently and deeply on the object of his desire, who can form an image with detailed clarity and hold it attentively in his mind for as long as he desires will experience the results of his thinking in physical manifestation. Practice daily concentrating on an object of your choice. You can start with something as simple as the tip of your finger. Set a timer for ten minutes, hold your right hand in front of you with your index finger extended, and gaze intently at the tip of your finger. Think only of your fingertip. When you are distracted by a vagrant thought, gently bring your attention back to the tip of your finger. Practice this for the duration of the ten minutes. You will find that daily exercise will strengthen your ability to hold your mind still and you will be able to concentrate for longer and longer periods of time.

The creative power of the mind starts with learning how to discipline the conscious mind. With our conscious mind we create or imagine what we want. The desire-seeds that are created in the conscious mind are planted in the fertile soil of the subconscious mind, which reproduces exactly what you have imaged. To have what you want in your life, therefore, means learning how to form the ideal in your mind with clarity and detail. With disciplined concentration, undivided attention, and a developed will to hold your attention still, you will be able to fashion strong thought-form images. You are then on your way to creating anything you desire.

"There's a way to do it better—find it."
— Thomas Edison

Steps

Have you ever wished that you had more control of the events in your life? Understanding the step-by-step process of visualization will offer you the keys to developing self control. When you know *how* visualization occurs you will learn how to identify within yourself the stage of the creative process you are experiencing at any time.

The first step in creating something new is a *stimulus* that comes from the completion of a goal. The nature of life and mind is motion, there is an everpresent flow of energy moving forward toward awareness. You can see this in the way a plant reaches toward the light, the way a baby reaches out to explore the environment. Thus, when you have completed a goal, the energy of life doesn't simply stop — it continues moving forward. You may experience this as a feeling of restlessness, perhaps anticipation, or being "high." When you are finishing a project, you are stimulated to imagine what to work on next. When you are close to completing the novel you are writing, you begin getting the bug to write another book. This stimulus is a glimpse into the next step of your evolution, the beginning of an idea of who you want to become next.

To illustrate, Susan is an actress who has been making her living acting in commercials and modeling. Recently, she filmed a series of commercials and received much praise from the people running the project. Susan became very anxious and restless as the project was nearing completion, finding herself irritable for no known reason. A friend asked Susan what was bothering her and Susan answered tearfully that she didn't know, but as she talked about her emotional state, she blurted out, "I just feel like I'm wasting my talent! I should be in New York!" It surprised her to hear the words tumble out of her mouth, but she realized that she had spent several weeks listening to the people on the film crew talk about their dreams to go to the Big Apple and pursue a career in television.   This stimulated her to imagine herself as a Broadway actress starring in plays, the original dream that had inspired her to become an actress. Since Susan was nearing the end of her job filming the commercials, she was ready to pursue her next creative endeavor.

The *desire* for more that is stimulated by completing a goal is a natural element within us. Creative desire is inherently ours. The thought, "I want" urges us to decide what to create next. When people are listless or pretend to themselves that they don't want anything, they are denying their most basic urge — the desire to create. What can you do to stimulate the powerful drive to create when it seems to be lost or forgotten? Knowing that the stimulus for a desire is the completion of a goal already accomplished, look to see what you have already done. This may take some practice, particularly if you have been taught not to toot your own horn, if you are used to taking yourself for granted. Oftentimes, when people do something well they ignore it and turn their attention instead to "problems" or what is going wrong in their lives.

John's example is somewhat typical. He was the leader of his church youth group, and had the remarkable ability to inspire the teenagers in the group. John was admired by many of the people in the congregation, because his charisma and encouragement stimulated the young people to become involved in community service projects. Many of these young people had been rebellious troublemakers before coming under John's wing. John didn't understand their admiration; he downplayed his ability to motivate the teenagers. One day the room in which the youth group held meetings sprung a leak. John was concerned about the problem because the church was not tremendously prosperous financially. He decided to have the members of the youth group raise the funds and donate their time to repair the roof. At first he met with doubt from the congregation. "These kids won't even pick up their rooms or take out the trash at home. You expect them to raise money *and* spend their time to work when they're not even getting paid?" John said yes. He spoke with the kids, painting a vision of the beautiful new roof they could build, how it would last for further generations, and how each person in the group could make their mark. He inspired them to believe in themselves, to see how important they were to many, many people. The teenagers were enthused. They generated lots of ideas about how to raise money, and even solicited help from their friends who were not members of the church. The experience prodded John to admit what he knew: how to inspire through communicating a clear vision, how to nurture another person's belief in themselves, how to produce group consciousness.

The "problem" of the leaky roof became an opportunity for John and the youth group to create, to expand their awareness of their capabilities, to go beyond their previous limitations. You can practice this yourself. When you think there is something going wrong in your life, see what you want to be different. If you think there's nothing you can do about it, stimulate your imagination by thinking, "If I could do something about it, what would it be?" Then start developing greater respect for your ability to create what you want by learning to see what you do well. It may take some practice to change the old way of thinking, that is, only looking at what you have done "wrong," to a new way that will be productive and fulfilling — observing what you have done right! At the end of every day, review your experiences. List what you have accomplished. List what you have completed. Write down even the smallest actions — "I smiled at the lonely-looking woman on the bus. I cleaned my room. I organized the files at work. I told my mother I love her when we spoke on the phone. I went to exercise class. I practiced the piano." Anything you have accomplished, completed, or produced counts. With daily practice, you will begin to see that you do have value and worth. This will help you to believe that you deserve to have what you want and that you are able to cause it to happen.

It is important to respect the power of *desire*. Many people are taught that desires are sinful or bad or selfish. A parent may teach an older sibling to sacrifice their own desires so that a younger sibling can have what they want. A mother may think that her own desires are not as important as those of her children, since her children need her. In the Buddhist tradition, "desirelessness" is considered to be a virtue. Many people feel ashamed or guilty when they desire. This is a fallacy. Everyone has desires. Desire is essentially divine, for it urges us to create and, therefore, to fulfill our destiny. The desire to improve life is the fuel for great inventors, leaders, statesmen, teachers, and writers. The desire to make the world a better place stimulates people to be responsible. The desire for happiness motivates people to change. The state of "desirelessness" results from fulfilling desires, not denying them. When you are hungry, you want food. After you have eaten a turkey dinner, you are full, you no longer desire to eat. Thus, you have attained desirelessness, at least for awhile.

The key to understanding desire is to examine what is most important to you. If you think it is selfish to satisfy your own wants, consider that there are many different kinds of desires. Physical, material desires are important to us, but realize that you could spend your entire life chasing after endless material desires that eventually become unsatisfying if they are not purposeful. You may have experienced this — you see an ad for a stationary bicycle that guarantees to shape your body in thirty days. You buy it, try it for a couple of weeks and then get bored, so it sits in your basement. Then you see an ad for a rowing machine that is new and improved, and the models demonstrating it are so fit you're sure it works. So you buy it, try it for a couple of weeks and then lose interest. It sits in the basement next to the bicycle. Then you see an advertisement for an exercise machine that simulates the action of cross-country skiing. This one promises to be the most complete exercise you can get, so you ask for this machine for your birthday and receive it as a gift. You use it for awhile, and then get tired of it. Where does it end up? In the basement, next to the other two machines. In order to create lasting satisfaction, be sure to develop purpose for your desires and to invest your time and energy in something lasting.

There are also desires that are less tangible. You may find it helpful to make a list of what is most important to you in this realm. For example, maybe you find that your close friends are valuable to you, and if you were to lose every material thing you own, you would still treasure your friends. Perhaps the support of your family is an essential element in your life. You may find that what brings you the greatest satisfaction is bettering yourself through education. When you look over the times you have been happiest, maybe you will discover that you have been involved in a creative activity, so you know that being creative is an important desire. Whatever is most important to you, you can produce it through using creative imagery.

The next step, then, in learning how to visualize effectively is making a *decision,* that is, clarifying from a more general desire the specific idea, thing, or object of your desire. Here is where you become a specialist. Here is where you decide that not only do you want a car, you want a particular color, model, price, with particular and specific features. This process of creating a specific, detailed object of desire will insure that you will have exactly what you want. In deciding what you want, understand that you have free will. With free will goes responsibility. Therefore, we are responsible for choosing how to create our lives and circumstances. The more willing you are to embrace and respect and use free will, the more powerful and creative you can become.

Oftentimes, people who are indecisive will say "I guess it wasn't meant to be" when an opportunity passes them by. For example, Eva was working as a nurse's aide, but her true heart's desire was to be an artist. She had drawn and sketched ever since she was a little girl, had taken a few art classes, and was quite talented artistically. Secretly Eva wanted to believe that she could become a professional artist, but she was also insecure. Eva found out that the local newspaper was looking for an illustrator, and she thought about applying for the job. But she had no professional experience, only twenty-five years of sketching in private notebooks and journals! Eva collected all her drawings together and called the newspaper to find out about the job. The receptionist told her that they were having interviews that week, and to come in. Eva mustered her courage and made plans to go in for an interview. But as she was ready to leave, she found that her car wouldn't start. Frustrated, but also a little relieved, Eva contacted the auto repair shop. They promised to work on the car and have it back the next day. The next day, Eva called the auto repair shop and was told that they didn't have the part needed for the repair, so the car wouldn't be ready until the following day. Eva figured that was all right, since there was still another day left for interviewing. But when she called to check on her car, she found out the part still hadn't arrived and her car would not be available until the following week. By this time it was late Friday afternoon, the week was practically gone, and Eva decided not to attempt the interview. Sighing to herself about the aborted attempts she said, "I guess it wasn't meant to be."

This statement is a falsehood! In Eva's case, her insecurity made her hesitant to interview for a position for which she feared she'd be rejected. When the problems arose with her car, had she been determined to go to the interview she could have explored other options: the bus, borrowing a friend's car, a taxicab. Instead, she rationalized defeat by pretending that circumstances beyond her control were a "sign" that she shouldn't go to the interview. There is no higher power that controls your life, no "ultimate destiny" that determines what will or won't be in your life. The creative power of your mind resides within *you,* in your conscious mind when you form clear, specific, detailed objects of your desires. Your subconscious mind will reproduce exactly what you have imagined in your conscious mind. When you imagine what you want, this is what you receive. When you imagine what you fear, you receive this as well.

The clearly defined, specific thought-form images you create in your conscious mind when you decide exactly what you want are like seeds that you plant in the fertile soil of your subconscious mind. To plant this seed you must release the thought from your mind. *Release* occurs when you remove your attention from the seed idea you have created. There are a number of ways to facilitate this process. One is to become involved in some other activity so that your attention is engaged elsewhere. For example, let us say that you have studied long and hard for a test at school. You have formed a clear ideal to perform well on the test so that you can apply to law school. Now it is ten o'clock in the evening and the exam is at eight o'clock the next morning. Rather than worrying and fearing, you can release your desire to succeed by watching a movie and then going to sleep. Another way to release is to use mental imagery, seeing your desire floating away on the tail of a kite in the wind, or encapsulated in a balloon that is carried off by the wind. You can image your desire as a ball that you are throwing for your subconscious mind to catch. In any case, it is important to activate the Universal Law of Believing and Knowing. The Law of Believing and Knowing states that when you have created a desire, this desire-thought is *real*. Thoughts are *things* and the completed, clear thought-form image is real. This is your belief. All it requires now is your physical activity for it to become physical. Believing in the reality of your thoughts is a very important element in creation. The belief that you give to your developing thought-form creations will help nurture them, will help them bloom. When your thought-form has become a physical reality, then you *know* its existence. All successful people have started with a firm belief in themselves and their creative ideas. Oftentimes they have faced prejudice or ridicule but they still persisted with their faith. Galileo is a good example of this: when the masses thought the world was flat, he maintained his belief that the world was round. Through experimentation and experience, the modern world now knows this fact. Believe in yourself, believe in the power of your creative ability, believe in the reality of thought, and soon you will know these truths.

When you doubt yourself, when you doubt that your thoughts are real, you sabotage the creative process of your mind. It would be like planting a healthy tomato seed in the ground, and because you doubt that it will ever amount to anything (after all, how could this tiny seed ever produce a plant, let alone one that will bear fruits that are good to eat?) you never water it, never pull the weeds, never give it light or attention. As healthy as the seed might be in the beginning, it will wither and die from lack of attention and care. Or perhaps you plant a healthy tomato seed and worry about whether it will grow, so every day you dig into the ground to look at it and see if it is growing. Robbed of the protective soil, separated from the life-giving nutrients in the ground, this tomato seed will also die. This is what happens when you create a good, sound thought-form creation and worry it to death! Give yourself a chance to discover how effective the creative process of your mind can be. Practice nurturing your budding desire-thoughts with loving thoughts of expectation, with hope, and with trust.

Releasing the object of your desire from your conscious mind and planting it in your subconscious mind causes the inner level developing work to begin. You will remember from studying the structure of the mind that your subconscious mind is part of the "inner you." The subconscious mind works as a developing agent, similar to the way a darkroom serves to develop a photograph. A photographer decides to capture a particular object on film to produce a photograph. The reflected light from the object is impressed on the film, and in the darkroom the chemicals interact with the film substance to draw out the image on the film. In the subconscious mind, a similar process takes place. There is an exchange of energies. The seed idea which you originally formed in your conscious mind as an object of desire has an attractive quality which draws toward it the mind substance within your mind. With the aid of an experienced teacher, you can learn how to consciously enter the inner levels of consciousness to participate in this process. But even without this kind of aid, you can have command of the developing process at work by creating solid thought-form images in your conscious mind and cooperating with the process that occurs in your subconscious mind. For now, be aware that cooperating with your own mind means trusting that you can have what you want when you are willing to invest yourself in fulfilling your desire. There is a mysterious magical universal law at work here, called the Law of Attraction. When you create a desire, its attractive power draws toward it all that you need to fulfill it! This is how "coincidence" occurs. Just when you are looking for a job you "happen" to meet someone who knows of the exact kind of job you are seeking. Or you have a hunch to drive a different way to work and see a help wanted sign on a store in which you've always wanted to work.

Know that there are always people and conditions and circumstances, there are always other minds, with desires compatible to yours. A simple way to see this in action is at a rummage sale. One person's junk is another person's treasure! When you want to clean out your attic and release old furniture and clothes, you are sure to attract to your sale someone who has been looking for exactly the piece of furniture or clothing you are discarding. When you do not have in your immediate environment the resources you need to fulfill your desires, there are *always* other minds, other people, who do have those resources. So you never have to wonder if you can fulfill a desire. All you need to do is create the clearly defined thought-form image, release it to your subconscious mind, and watch for the signs of your manifestation so that you can cooperate and respond. Trust in the power of the Law of Attraction and look for ways to cooperate with your own desires.

"To desire is to obtain,
to aspire is to achieve."
— James Allen,
As A Man Thinketh

Ideals and Goals

Many people find the idea awesome that we can receive whatever we desire. The creative ability is indeed a great power, privilege, and responsibility. With a limited amount of time — perhaps eighty to one hundred years in a lifetime — it is important to use discrimination and care in deciding what to create. It would be a shame to be on your deathbed thinking that you had wasted your time and wishing you had done things differently. What makes life worth living? What are your greatest dreams? These are questions that may seem ponderous but are well worth considering.

Some people are afraid of their creative power, afraid to make a mistake or a wrong choice. It helps to realize that the decision-making process is one of learning. Every time you decide what you want and go about creating it, you will learn more about how your creative faculties work. When you are establishing purposes for your creations, you need not fear making "wrong" choices, for every experience will add to your awareness of how to create more effectively. Learning how to be decisive will aid you to use your time and creative power most efficiently.

For example, when I was in college I was having great difficulty deciding what to choose as a major. I had the overwhelming desire to do something important with my life and a sense of urgency to choose a major that would provide me with the perfect means of self expression. I couldn't decide what career would provide the best vehicle for me to fulfill the mission I was "supposed" to do, because I hadn't decided exactly what I wanted to do. I knew that I was creative, and I knew that I found satisfaction in playing the piano, in designing miniatures and craft projects. I knew that I loved writing in all forms. I knew that I liked to teach. I had, at one time, imagined being an architect but had not chosen to study courses in physics and calculus that were requirements for entering architecture school. I thought about being a lawyer, for I was an avid fan of the Perry Mason television show and I imagined being able to right the injustices of the world through being a lawyer.

The difficulty I was having revolved around the awareness that committing myself to one major necessitated eliminating the others. If I chose to major in music, I would not be a writer, teacher, architect, artist or lawyer. If I chose English, I would not be a musician, architect, artist or lawyer. If I chose law, I would not be a writer, architect, musician or artist. And so forth. I wanted to be able to do everything, but in my indecisiveness I wasn't choosing anything and so I ended up fulfilling *none* of these desires. Finally, I determined that I had to choose something, and in the process of pursuing that one thing I would find out what it was what would fulfill me. I also determined that I could pursue one career for a period of time and then pursue another; but if I continued to wait for the "perfect" answer I would end up with nothing.

I finally decided to choose English as my major. I figured that would give me the greatest probability of pursuing a writing career, and would also enable me to teach. It would give me a good well-rounded view of the world from many perspectives. After one semester in which I had four English literature classes, I discovered that many of the English professors at the university had been teaching for years, and had become bored with their teaching. Not all; I had one professor who introduced me to poetry and to Shakespeare in a dramatic and dynamic manner that sparked a love which I still have today. But many of the other teachers in the English department were bored with their work, dry, and uninteresting. I found out that for me, education was very important, and I did not view an undergraduate education as a career training school; I wanted it to be a process of stimulation and expansion. This discovery arose only after having chosen English as my major.

I could have condemned myself for making a mistake, for choosing the wrong major. Instead, I looked at my options. I still had time to change my major, and I had taken enough classes in different areas to enable me to graduate with all my distribution requirements even if I chose another major. I examined my experiences in school and decided that it was important to me to choose a major which would give me some practical life experiences and which had a high percentage of teachers who loved what they were teaching.

I was taking one class in Women's Studies. The professor of that class was enthusiastic, dedicated to her ideals, and willing to extend herself beyond the minimum requirement of teaching her class. I decided to enroll in some other Women's Studies classes to see if that attitude prevailed. Since Women's Studies was a relatively new program at that time, and since the instructors of Women's Studies classes were all teachers who voluntarily committed extra hours to the Women's Studies program, I found an unusually high degree of commitment, dedication, enthusiasm, and giving in this department. It was on that basis that I chose Women's Studies for my major.

In this decision-making process I discovered more about what I wanted. In the beginning of making my choice, I was paralyzed by the fear of making a wrong decision. As it turned out, my first choice of major was not exactly what I wanted, but until I committed myself to a course of action, I did not have the experience or knowledge to more accurately determine what would be most fulfilling. When I made a choice, I found out that it was, indeed, a "wrong" choice for my ideal, but I would have never known that had I stayed in my original indecision! I also found out more exactly what I wanted from making a choice, and found out how to ask better questions to arrive at a better answer. Thus, it was a learning process which enabled me to choose a wise course of study.

When you have difficulty in being decisive it is often because you have forgotten your origins. Remember that the first step in creating anything is recognizing when you have completed a goal. Practice admitting your accomplishments and being thankful for what you have already achieved and received.

Many children are taught to "count their blessings" before going to sleep at night. Counting your blessings is admitting what you have and giving thanks for it. This is an excellent practice and one which will aid you to identify the sources of abundance in your life. Make a list of everything and everyone in your life for which you are grateful, including the smallest to the greatest. In this manner you will discover how wealthy you are. You don't create something from nothing; you always create something from something. That is, you use what you already have in a new way to create improved conditions in your life.

Your "grateful" list may include talents, skills and abilities you have. For example, you may be grateful for your reasoning abilities, your generosity, your quick mind, your intelligence, your compassion. You may be grateful for your calligraphy skills, your skill with automotive mechanics, your ability to articulate thoughts in words. You may also include people in your life for whom you are grateful: your parents, your friends, your teachers. You may be grateful for conditions such as a steady job, beautiful weather, a dependable car, etc. The more specifically you describe the people, places, and objects for which you are thankful, the more awareness you will have of the resources in your hands. I know a woman named Betty who used this method to begin healing after her husband died. Betty was very much in love with her husband and depended on him for emotional and financial support. When he died of a sudden heart attack, Betty was devastated. She had been married since she was nineteen years old, and now at the age of fifty-nine, she did not even want to live without him. Betty had to do something, so she listed everything for which she was grateful. First, her five wonderful children, who offered her love and support and encouragement through the grieving process. Next, her house which was ample for her needs, in good repair, and a comforting reminder of the home she had shared with her husband. Then she listed the financial support her husband had provided in insurance and benefits and savings. Then Betty started giving attention to herself. She was thankful for her ability to sew, which kept her mind occupied. She was grateful for the many friends she had made at church, people who were very willing to go out of their way to help her. She was thankful for the courage and strength she had developed throughout her life, especially during times when her family was in trouble. As Betty listed these items, she started coming out of her depression and realized that she had a tremendous amount of love she wanted to give. Her husband's death had left a void in her life because she needed someone to whom she could give her love. Betty decided to become more involved in her church activities. Every year the church collected used clothing to distribute to needy families at Christmas time. Some of the clothes were torn, and Betty volunteered her time to sew the clothing that needed repair. She discovered great joy in giving, and also made some new friends who were involved in the project. One of these new friends introduced Betty to her brother who had been recently divorced. Betty and this man grew to like one another and eventually married.

Betty's story is not unusual. At first, all she could perceive was loss — the loss of her husband, her dearest friend, her companion, her security, her comfort. By evaluating what she still had within and around her, Betty discovered she had not lost love. In fact, she revealed to herself how much love she had and how much she wanted to give it! Fulfilling her desire to give through service expanded Betty's world, and she found new resources. Betty became happier as she shared her talents, and her happiness helped her draw into her life a man with whom she could share the greatest treasure she owned — her love. Every time you respond to a desire, you will uncover resources that were previously unavailable to you. In this way you will find that you can fulfill desires that at one time may have seemed unattainable.

Once you have admitted what *you already have,* you will be stimulated to identify what you want. Desires can be physical or mental. Both are important. As long as we have a physical body for experiencing and a physical world for a schoolroom, we have physical desires. As long as we are spiritual beings inhabiting these bodies, we have desires for spiritual progression. Learn how to discriminate between needs and desires, for physical desires can be endless. What do you really *need* for the physical sustenance you require? What do you *want* for peace, contentment and security? What will provide permanent satisfaction and what will provide temporary relief, giving way to a new desire to be fulfilled? The more purposeful you are, the more contentment you will develop as you create.

Deciding what you want will give you a direction. There are limitless opportunities to create and countless desires to be fulfilled. Only you can determine in what direction you will point your mind. "Brainstorming" is a good method to use to begin deciding what you want. Brainstorming is a process of writing down every possible alternative, without placing any limitations or restrictions on it. This can be done alone or in a group. The principle of brainstorming is that anything goes, no matter how wild, impractical, or crazy it may seem. You are giving your mind an opportunity to expand, and especially when a group of people brainstorm together, each person's ideas can stimulate the others' imaginations. Only after all the possibilities have been exhausted, after everything is out on paper, do you take the next step, which is becoming specific, weeding out the impractical ideas, delineating how to make the ideas work that have been thrown on the table. In this process, ask yourself, How? When? Where? In what manner? How much? Who? to become specific about the ways in which the ideas that have been generated can work.

Here is an example. Suppose you have decided that you want a new job. You have already determined that you are thankful for the following in the job you currently have: decent pay, flexible hours, pleasant people with whom you work, short traveling time. You have decided that what you want to add is a greater challenge for your skills and talents, for you have become bored with your work. So you start to brainstorm what you enjoy doing: design, creative projects, working with people, public speaking...and in the process you start to think, "I'm not a good enough speaker, there are no jobs available for artists." *Stop that thought!* This is the time for expansion, for putting out and imagining *all* possibilities with no holds. So continue with your dreams: writing, coordinating projects, leadership activities...keep on writing until you have written everything that you enjoy doing. *Now* begin to delineate how this can fit together in a particular job. In this case you may need to do some research. Perhaps you have never considered how these varied talents and interests could fit together in one job. Use your resources. Go to the library. Visit career counseling centers and talk with a guidance counselor. Interview different companies to find out what types of positions are available. Talk with people you know who are employed in fields where they use talents you want to use. In this information-gathering process you are defining *how* and *where* and *when* the different elements fit together.

Once you have collected all the information you need, you can create a clearly defined, specific thought-form image using images from memory, such as images from places you visited, and your imagination to put together in a new way exactly the kind of position you desire. You may not even have a name or job title, but you will have all the elements put together. For example, you may decide to become a creative consultant for an advertising firm in which you can speak to people to find out what their advertising needs are, design brochures, put together educational seminars to fill their needs, coordinate the people involved in the seminars, and promote your own services. In this way you are employing the different skills and talents and interests you have in one position.

The process of creating a clearly defined specific *object of desire* is one of the most important elements in visualization, for it is how you plant seeds in your subconscious mind. This is the forming of your ideal or goal. Your subconscious mind cannot decide what it wants; it can only reproduce what you give it. The more specific you are, the more exactly you will create what you desire. In creating a thought-form image, you employ your five senses. Imagine what your ideal will look like, sound like, smell like, taste like, and feel like. When you can define it and describe it will all five senses you know it is complete.

Often, you will hear people say, "I can't *imagine* having a job that will include all those skills." It's no wonder they don't have what they want in life! In order to have it you must imagine it. If you "can't" imagine it, practice using your senses to stretch your imagination. You can exercise this with any goal or ideal you create. You can even go to places that are similar to what you want, in order to gather information through your senses to store in your memory banks. For example, suppose you are creating the image of a new car and you are having difficulty imagining the smell of the new upholstery. Go visit an automobile dealer and test drive a car like the one you want. Look at the color, shape, design. Feel the steering wheel under your hands, feel how the road feels as you drive it. Smell the upholstery, giving special attention to this sense so that you can remember it. Hear the hum of the engine and the sound of the stereo cassette player in the car. Collect all the information so that when you are creating your object of desire you can draw upon these memory images. The more you practice giving your undivided attention to your five senses in your daily life, the easier it will be for you to use them to create mental pictures.

Using your five senses to describe your objects of desire is a sure-fire way to believe in the reality of thoughts. When you can imagine a goal with all of your senses it is easy to *believe* that it will manifest. When you have difficulty believing in something, look to see how clear your image is. Is it vague and unspecific? Then strive to make it clear, detailed, and concrete. A number of years ago I started observing and listening to people who had difficulty believing in the presence of a God or Supreme Being. When I asked these people how they would describe the Supreme Being they didn't believe in, invariably I got responses like, "It's indescribable." "A power." "A force." Their images were vague. The people who *did* believe in a God or Supreme Being had much more concrete images: " A kind, loving, grandfatherly-type being who watches over me." "A warm, protective, enveloping light that feels like a secure hug." When someone has a clear image it is easy to believe in its existence. When it is vague, there is nothing to believe in!

If you have difficulty believing in something, then, *create* the image with detailed clarity. In this way you will create faith. This will give you something specific and concrete toward which you can direct your energies. When it is complete and clear and you can describe it with your senses, you can release it to your subconscious mind for development. You will not have to worry about it because you will know it is a good seed. In the movie *Fiddler on the Roof,* Tevye's daughters each choose a suitor and ask their father for his blessing. Blessing a union such as a marriage means recognizing that it will be productive. When you give any idea your blessing, you know that this idea is complete and whole and will work. This does not mean that it is completed in physical form, but that the visualized image is whole and complete and all it takes is your physical activity to cause it to become physical. You know that the physical activity will produce the desired results because the thought-form image is whole. When your thought forms are complete you can rest from the work done in creation, which means you no longer need to mold the image in your thinking. You have created a clear and complete thought-form image and now it is up to your subconscious mind to do its inner level development work.

When you are highly creative, you cannot create everything you desire in your life all at once. There is a need to learn how to prioritize what is most important to accomplish first. Prioritizing your desires is practicing proper perspective, enabling you to have everything you want by wisely judging what will bring you the greatest peace and contentment. Knowing what you want is the first step.

"The highest reward for a man's toil
is not what he gets for it
but what he becomes by it."
— John Ruskin

Purpose

Have you ever *really* wanted something, only to find once you had it that you felt empty? Or perhaps have you discovered that the material objects you thought would bring you peace and contentment only brought you bills and worry? If these are common experiences for you, it indicates a need to understand how to create *purposes* for the goals you set.

We have introduced you to a sure-fire formula for success: Ideal, Purpose, and Activity. Purpose is perhaps the least understood of this three-step formula. Purpose provides motivation, purpose offers the peace and contentment and fulfillment we all desire, purpose is how you become more creative. When purpose is present we are alive, our creations are a source of happiness, we are in love with what we are doing. When purpose is missing, we become depressed, anxious, and unsatisfied.

A common example of lack of purpose occurs with post-partum depression. Physical considerations and hormone imbalances aside, it is common for a woman to experience a depression after giving birth. Why? For nine months she has anticipated the arrival of her child, has prepared the nursery, has shared the excitement with family and friends, has bought clothes and toys. She has prepared herself to receive a new entity into her life. But has she prepared herself to become a new woman? Has she imagined herself as a mother, what qualities she will be giving from within herself, what changes she will incorporate into her identity and embrace in her soul? For example, she may intend to use the new experience to become more giving, loving, and attentive. Has she imagined how she will practice being a parent? How the child will affect her career, her marriage? These questions are purposeful, these questions will stimulate her awareness of *who she will become.* In order to fully receive a new experience in your life, it means preparing not only for the physical changes but for the mental, emotional and spiritual changes as well. These changes describe purpose.

Every physical object and physical experience represents a mental or spiritual quality. For example, money represents power and value. Think about this. When you understand how to use monetary resources wisely, you have a great amount of power and awareness of your value. You have access to greater opportunity and experience freedom because you can make more choices. For example, you can become educated, travel to distant places, entertain friends, save for the future, and so on. When you think you do not have enough money, or when you identify with being "broke," you are powerless, you think of yourself as worthless. The money itself does not give you power and value. It is your *use* of money that determines how aware you are of power and value. Here is a good example which illustrates how I learned about freedom and power through understanding the use of money. I was in a situation, rare for me, in which I did not have much extra money. I had a job which earned enough to pay my rent and basic living expenses, but I found myself scared of coming up short, particularly if there was a car repair or some other large expense. I started keeping records of every penny I spent. This was enlightening, as it showed me the "small" ways that I wasted money that could be better used elsewhere. I discovered that every day I was purchasing coffee from the cafeteria at work, one cup in the morning and one in the afternoon. Each cup cost 50¢, which meant that I was spending $1.00 a day to drink a couple of cups of coffee. Working five days a week, I was spending $5.00 a week, and over $20.00 a month. Twenty dollars was enough to pay an electric bill or to provide meals for a week! I realized that this seemingly insignificant 50¢ a day was adding up, so I bought a can of coffee, brewed it at home, and took a Thermos with me to work. This was not a huge change, but it made a difference. As I watched the other ways that I wasted pennies I found out that I had great abundance in the conditions already present in my life. I didn't need to win the lottery or have a miraculous windfall to have greater wealth. The money itself did not give me power or restrict it; it was my use of reasoning and creativity in choosing how to spend money that gave me freedom.

I discovered another important truth in this period in my life. One day a group of women from my office were talking about going out for lunch. I decided I would rather save my money and eat the sandwich I brought from home. I overheard one of the other women saying, "I can't go, I'm broke." These words shocked me, because I knew that I did not think of myself as "broke," I was making a choice about how I wanted to use the monetary resources available to me, and I had a sense of freedom in being able to make that choice. I was content with my choice because I knew what I intended to produce with it — I was aware that there are always options in life and that making choices is a fact of life. Deciding how to use the money I had available became a creative endeavor, one which continually challenged me to examine my values, what I determined to be most important and worthwhile. The woman who was "broke" was identifying with being limited, restricted, and trapped. The image she projected was like that of an animal whose spirit is broken. The money — or more accurately, her fear of not having enough — was controlling how she viewed herself and her life. A better way to approach any condition in life is to view it as an opportunity to learn and to create.

In defining purposes for your ideals, ask yourself what the "thing" you desire represents or symbolizes in your life, your awareness, and your identity. You develop purposefulness as you determine how to *use* the thing you desire. There was a young woman named Meryl who had just started attending college. Meryl loved music, and in her parents' house there was a good quality stereo system with a wide variety of records. When she moved away from home, she missed being able to play any music she wanted and started considering buying a stereo of her own. Meryl was a thrifty child, and she had been saving her allowance and baby-sitting money for years, but she had never even thought about spending it. Now she thought hard about spending her money to buy an expensive item. Meryl did have a good record collection which she had built over the years, and she was uneasy about playing her good records on her friends' stereos, because most of them were not very high quality and she had seen how a needle could scratch a record and ruin it. She finally decided to purchase her own system so that she could listen to music and have the kind of quality she desired. She shopped around, listened to many salespeople, took a friend with her who was a disc jockey at the campus radio station and who had a lot of knowledge about sound equipment, and finally settled on the turntable, receiver, and speakers she wanted. She also bought the highly-recommended accessories for cleaning and taking care of records. The system was very expensive and Meryl spent almost all of her savings, but she figured it was a good investment as the equipment would last for a long time. When she got the system set up, she was very finicky about caring for it, and would not let any of her friends touch it because she was afraid it would get destroyed. She cleaned all the records, she made sure that there was no dust anywhere near the equipment, and she asked people to stay away from the turntable because any jarring could cause the needle to jump and scratch a record.

After awhile, protecting her records and equipment from harm became a burden to Meryl. Her friends respected her wishes, but it was not much fun to be around her because she was so worried about ruining her stereo. Meryl did not even enjoy listening to her records much any more because her attention was consumed with cleaning them, with ensuring that the dust cover was always on the turntable, with putting everything back in order. After awhile the equipment sat unused in her room because it was too much work to use it! Meryl had forgotten her purpose for purchasing the stereo in the first place — she loved music, loved to listen to it, and loved to use it as a way of bringing people together. The reason she spent her money was to add enjoyment to her life and to bring pleasure to others, but this original purpose got lost in her unhealthy attachment to the equipment itself. It is important to know that physical things will always deteriorate — this is the nature of physical existence. They do deserve care, and it is important to respect and use what you own. But what is the point of having something in your life if you are so afraid of it getting dirty or deteriorating that you don't even use it? Knowing *why* you want it and what purpose it serves is the way to use most fully what you have.

With every goal you create, you are involved in activity. The satisfaction you derive from creating goals is not in the end result, it is in the process of creation. While you are in the process of creating your object, circumstance, or thing, you are becoming someone new. You are adding awareness to yourself, you are developing new skills or honing ones you have already developed. You are building qualities in yourself. This process of *becoming* is purpose and it is how you become fulfilled. Ask yourself what kind of person you are and what kind of person you want to be. What character traits do you admire? Do you exhibit these yourself? Are there ones you want to add? There are hundreds of thousands of qualities you could develop in yourself. Here are some examples: compassion, love, determination, discipline, integrity, beauty, trust, intelligence, responsibility, dependability, honesty, faith, honor, ingenuity.

When you give attention to the qualities you intend to produce you build spiritual maturity. We are here to learn how to create. The understandings of Universal Law and Truth and the awareness of qualities that aid us to create we store in our subconscious mind, or soul. This is why, when we are purposeful in our creations, we feel satisfied and fulfilled — we are filling our soul full of understanding and awareness! Being purposeful is how we live our highest ideals, how we become our most inspired and lofty image. Because our true nature is creative, every time we purposefully create our highest Self, we experience the joy of expansion. We are no longer lonely, for we are discovering more completely who we are, what we are made of, what we are capable of. Psychologist Abraham Maslow calls this creative act and the accompanying "feeling" a peak experience. We experience the peak of our capabilities every time we strive to improve ourselves.

When we embrace challenges, we grow into a new and greater self. We may be adding new qualities to ourselves or developing skills we have already mastered to some degree.

Creative imagination is an important element to use when a situation seems hard or difficult. By imagining becoming an improved self, that is, keeping in mind a high ideal, we are motivated to reach beyond the limitations we have previously accepted. Here is an example. In my late teens I went on a backbacking trip with a group of people. At that time I was not physically fit, and I had never gone camping or backpacking. Many of the other people in the group had greater experience and skill. We were in New Hampshire, hiking in the woods with packs upon our backs. The scenery was beautiful — lush trees, many different kinds of birds, lizards, chipmunks and other forest creatures. It was late spring, and the air was cool, the sun warm. At first I was enjoying the hike as we ascended a path along a babbling brook. After about an hour of hiking, however, I started to get tired. I was out of breath, my legs were sore, I was tired, and the trail seemed to go on forever. The woodland beauty escaped me as I focused more upon my physical pain. I had a choice to make — to continue in misery or find some way to turn this into an enjoyable experience! One of the more experienced hikers told me that the best way to develop endurance was to focus on one step at a time, to take small steps rather than large strides, and to keep moving rather than stopping for breaks. This man was slightly overweight and his backpack was much heavier than mine, but he was not winded and seemed full of energy. He did walk slowly, unlike some of the other hikers who sprinted ahead like the hare in Aesop's Fable, "The Tortoise and the Hare." I took his advice, focusing on each step. As I stepped on each rock, I looked at the surroundings and found that I had renewed energy from receiving the beauty of nature's grandeur that was around me. I also concentrated on building strength and endurance within myself, for I knew that it was not just physical endurance I needed, it was the attitude that each small step is motion toward the end result. Walter and I fell behind the rest of the group, walking step by step, slowly and steadily, and I did experience a kind of slow and steady energy upon which to draw. Eventually we came upon the rest of the group, sitting by the side of the trail, sweating and panting, needing to rest from their over-exertion of energy. Walter smiled as we passed them, nodding his head, and we moved on.

Soon we came to a breathtaking sight. The trees had been getting shorter as we ascended, and Walter told me that the higher altitude starved them of needed oxygen and that eventually they would cease growing completely. We got to the place called the tree line — where the trees stopped growing. Previously we could see the forest as we walked, but suddenly we could see the bald rock face of the mountain clear to the top. We could also see the peaks of the mountains in the surrounding range. It was like coming up to heaven — everything opened up in a vast panorama. I felt a tremendous surge of energy and wanted to run up the rocks the rest of the way, but Walter reminded me of the step-by-step principle. I was glad I listened to him, because scaling the rock the rest of the way required concentration and balance. When we reached the top, we rested. I could see for hundreds of miles — peak after peak. It was spectacular.

The trip down was a little easier than the way up, especially since I had learned how to conserve my energy, to breathe properly, and most important, to take one step at a time. This experience has aided me in many other endeavors in life, when I have been tempted to give up, when a goal has seemed out of reach, when I have not been able to see the way to accomplish an ideal. I remember taking one step at a time, and remember coming to the tree line where the accumulation of all those small steps opened up a new perspective, much broader and more expansive than before. The situation that at first seemed hard turned into a challenge that aided me to discover the secret to perseverance.

Any experience in life can be used to develop new strength or skill. It is beneficial to ask yourself, "How can I improve upon this? What else can I learn?" I have used this when writing. I have always loved to write, from the time I was a young child writing letters or poetry to writing essays in junior high school to scholarly papers in college. It is challenging to me to explore new kinds of writing or to find new avenues for written expression. For example, a teacher of mine has a degree in journalism from a prestigious Midwestern school. She taught me about how to interview someone, a skill that was new to me. In doing interviews, I had opportunities to learn how to listen, to be attentive, to respond to the person being interviewed. I also learned how to observe, to capture their essence not only from their words but from their gestures, mannerisms, environment, form of dress. Even though writing is a skill I have practiced, the new situation provided me with ways to add to the skill and to add to my understanding of relating with people. Similarly, in learning how to write poetry, I was challenged to go beyond describing my ideas with intellectual concepts and to use sensual description. This also stimulated me to expand my perception, to look at things from a different perspective, to observe more closely and to receive information I had previously passed over. Being purposeful helps us to look for something new in any experience, which keeps us fresh, curious, and full of joy in life.

Furthermore, when we are purposeful we learn that success is ours to command. Physical things are temporary, and physical success is also temporary. But the mental qualities and spiritual awareness we build is permanent. When we are learning discipline, for example, we can apply this in any area of life. We can apply it to become an excellent athlete, master the piano, to practice meditation, or for any endeavor we choose. Therefore, when we are learning to become who we desire, we have the security of knowing those mental and spiritual abilities are ours to use eternally. They go wherever we go. They become a permanent part of us the more we use and understand them. This gives us a maturity, an inner strength that comes from knowing how to be productive and how to cause what we desire. It gives us self-possession. We have the confidence and security that we can handle anything. It also enables us to be more compassionate with others, for as we build qualities of understanding we realize we are connected to one another as member of the human race. The more we understand how Universal Law and Truth operate, the more aware we become of our relationship with one another. We are each individuals, with our own experiences and thoughts, but our minds and spirits are created the same way and operate according to the same principles. The more Self awareness and understanding we develop, therefore, the more we can understand our brothers and sisters.

It is a curious paradox that the more we understand who we are, the more we realize our uniqueness while recognizing our similarity with others. It is our quest not only to discover what makes us unique, but to create our individuality. We are individuals with free will and intelligence. Each choice we make sets up conditions for us to change our identity. There is a motivating force within each of us that spurs us on to create and to understand our Selves. This is called *ego*. The word "ego" in Latin means "I AM". Ego is our individuality, our identity. The ego motivates us to create our individuality. Depending upon how much awareness we have of our true nature, how aware we are of our spiritual nature, we create with greater or lesser productivity. The productive use of ego is to listen to our thoughts and choose to create with those that align with the goals of becoming our best and highest Self. How do I want to influence others? In what ways can I make a difference? How do I want to serve? These are productive questions to ask and will aid you in creating a direction which will benefit yourself and others. They will stimulate you to draw upon what you want to give. When you focus upon giving, you will always receive greater awareness of who you are. An undisciplined ego will motivate you for temporary physical gains. For example, creating a bigger house to keep up with the Joneses is a misuse of ego, for you are identifying yourself in comparison with someone else, rather than comparing yourself with your own achievements and aspirations. When you are thinking of yourself as "better" or "worse" than the other person, as "higher" or "lower," these are misuses of ego.

There are many ways that the ego can be used for motivation. These change according to our states of awareness. The most elevated use of the ego is when we choose to create for the purpose of becoming a better creator, for developing greater awareness of our best and highest self. Another use of ego is commonly referred to as ego motivation. A person who operates from this stage of awareness is motivated by status, power, especially by how they are looked at or seen by others. This motivation can be very powerful for producing physical results, but the satisfaction from them is short-lived. A third use is motivation by the senses. A person who eats compulsively, who chases after relationships for sexual gratification, who successfully sells only for money is motivated by physical reward. Because the physical world changes rapidly, this motivation is also very temporary, for the satisfaction of physical desire soon gives way to another physical desire.

Let's examine these different motivations with the example of Joe, Larry, and Steve. All three were salesmen for the ABC Company. Joe had worked for the company for years, but he still continually struggled to make ends meet. He met each day with a heavy heart, for he hated rejection and feared losing sales. But he had five children and a house to maintain, so he worked day after day, year after year, to bring home a paycheck. His wife was distressed by his depression, because he would come home from work and lose himself in the television until falling into bed exhausted. She kept telling him that the money was not the most important thing in life and encouraged him to find a job he would enjoy, but Joe was convinced that he wouldn't make enough money at another type of job and stayed in his same, dull routine. Larry was recently transferred to ABC Company from XYZ Company where he had been the top salesperson until a new recruit outclassed him too many times. In a fit of rage, Larry left the company because he couldn't stand being second. He was highly charismatic and made many friends in the company as well as making friends with clients, but he was also very dependent upon his supervisor's approval to be satisfied with his work. At times Larry was driven to make sales and exuded enthusiasm and passion for his job, but at other times he was angry, sullen and fitful, particularly when he thought that he wasn't being adequately praised or recognized. Steve started working for ABC Company when he learned that their products were energy efficient and economical. He investigated the company's ideals and found out that their philosophy was to help people help themselves. Steve didn't know much about sales, but he did believe in the company and was sincere in communicating with the customers. In a short period of time, Steve learned how to listen better to the customers, how to communicate more completely and clearly the benefits of the products he sold, and he was inspired to keep growing. His supervisor suggested that he begin training new recruits since he had improved so much in a short period of time. When Steve was teaching the new salespeople how to listen, how to communicate, and how to respond to the customers' needs, Steve discovered that the principles he used in sales could be applied to other areas of his life, like with his children. He had been having some trouble communicating with his teenage daughters but through teaching someone else how to do what he was doing in sales, he discovered universal truths that worked for him to become a better father.

Joe's motivation was for physical gain, Larry was motivated by a desire to impress others, and Steve was motivated by a desire to improve himself and his world. Steve discovered a Universal Law of Abundance: when you aid others to abundance you have abundance yourself. Through learning and sharing his discoveries with others, his own life was dramatically improved.

Developing your awareness of yourself as a creative being gives you opportunities for joy in your physical life, for even in the creation of physical things and circumstances you can become a better person. Knowing what those things and circumstances represent to you enables you to use them to the fullest and to know when the purpose for the desire has been fulfilled. This is helpful for releasing attachments to experiences that are no longer productive or creative. For example, how do you know when it is time to end a relationship? Ask yourself if it has fulfilled its purpose. Are you still using the association to learn about giving and receiving? Are you still practicing warmth, compassion, or other qualities? Then it is still useful and productive. But suppose you are only using the relationship for physical comfort and security and you are no longer actively practicing to develop qualities in yourself nor are you aiding your partner to grow. In that case, the association is no longer purposeful.

To develop purpose, it is useful to think about what you want to give to any situation and what you want to receive. I have heard many people say, "I give, give, give, but I never receive."

This isn't possible! Giving and receiving are intertwined, and when there is complete giving there is also complete receiving. Giving initiates the cycle, so when you feel depleted, look to see where you are holding back or how you can give in different ways. You may find that you are giving to be noticed or appreciated, which means that your intention is actually to "get" something — praise or recognition — rather than truly desiring to give. It will help to ask yourself, "How can I improve this situation?" "How will I make this world a better place?" The more you practice giving, the more *awareness* you will receive of who you are and what you have to offer. In our earlier example, Steve discovered what he knew about listening and responding to needs by giving to another salesperson. Steve received a greater awareness and through applying that to his situation with his daughters, he also received greater understanding of love.

I knew a dentist who had a high ideal for his practice. He wanted to teach preventive dentistry to help people live healthier lives with healthier mouths. But Dr. Carson found himself very frustrated and irritable much of the time, because none of the people on his staff seemed interested in his ideal. Furthermore, Dr. Carson had a lot of patients who didn't care about their teeth and who would not follow his instructions for tending to them. Dr. Carson was unhappy with his life and thought about changing occupations. He asked himself, "What is my purpose? What am I here to do?" Then he remembered his ideals when he originally became a dentist. He wanted to teach seminars and treat people who wanted to participate in their own health care. The purpose for his choice of dentistry was to aid people to improve their lives, not simply to pull or fill teeth that had been ruined from neglect. Dr. Carson thought about what he wanted to give to the world, and communicated this with his staff. Two of the employees were eager to share in his dream but the other two remained indifferent. Dr. Carson replaced them with new employees who also wanted to teach the patients how to care for their teeth. Then he spoke with all of his patients about the conditions he had for treating them: they needed to brush their teeth three times a day, floss, and have their teeth cleaned twice a year. Without this regular treatment he knew their teeth would become diseased. Some of the patients agreed to his conditions, others made it clear they would continue with their old habits. Dr. Carson told the latter that they would need to find another dentist. He became much more fulfilled and received the kind of patients who wanted to learn what he had to offer, because he had committed himself to giving what he knew to be true.

Oftentimes I hear people ask the question, "What is my purpose in life?" There is one purpose in life, to learn and grow. There are many opportunities to learn and many choices through which we develop a unique identity. When we are considering different choices in life, knowing what we want to give helps us to discriminate what is the best situation. There is one ideal, which we all share, and that is for us to create. As we use our physical life experiences to learn how to become more creative, we are fulfilling our purposes in life. We are happier, healthier, more abundant, content, and at peace.

"Cherish your visions; cherish your ideals,
cherish the music that stirs in your heart,
the beauty that forms in your mind,
the loveliness that drapes your purest thought,
for out of them will grow all beautiful conditions,
all heavenly environment; of these, if you but remain
true to them, your world will at last be built."
— James Allen, As A Man Thinketh

Activity

The greatest dreams of man often die in doubt, fear, hesitation, and passivity. A well-known manufacturer of athletic shoes recently has run a series of advertisements showing people engaged in different sports activities with the caption, "Just do it." Easier said than done! Why is it difficult to *act* on the ideas you have? Why do people procrastinate and then berate themselves for wasting their lives?

Oftentimes, when there is difficulty with physical activity to reach an ideal, it is because there has been insufficient *mental* activity to create the desired thought-form image. We are mental creatures first, and our physical bodies merely serve as residences for the activity of our minds. When there is hesitation physically, in all cases it is because there has been mental hesitation first.

The secret of "follow through" is to create a complete mental image of the desired results. When you have completely formed the ideal with visualization, it is relatively easy to determine what steps of action to take to cause the ideal to manifest. When the thought form is incomplete, it is no wonder we hesitate to take a step.

For example, let us suppose that the object of your desire is a new job. Every morning you resolve to wake up early and search for the job. But you find yourself shutting off the alarm for "just 10 minutes" which turns into a half hour, then sleeping just a little more, and then it is too late to go out. Or you find a million and one little distractions to keep you from going out job hunting — balancing your checkbook, cleaning out a closet, ironing clothes. If this sounds like you, examine the object of your desire. Have you visualized exactly what kind of job you want? Have you imagined yourself working in a new position and doing it well? Have you specifically imaged the skills, talents, and abilities you will be doing on your new job? This kind of detailed thought-form image will provide fuel for you to go out and look for a job. It will aid you in knowing what resources to use to plan your steps of action. It will give you a point of reference for knowing when the job for which you interview matches the object of your desire.

Once you have created a clearly defined thought-form image and know that it is complete because you have identified it with all of your senses, you are ready for the next step of mental activity. This is known as broadcasting. Your mind is very powerful and just as a radio station can broadcast programs which reach for hundreds of miles, so your mind can broadcast mental vibration, or thought forms, which reach out to other minds, and when another is receptive to your broadcast this sets up a mental attraction. Your subconscious mind is linked with every other subconscious mind, even when consciously you do not see or know how your desire will manifest. Your subconscious mind is like the genie in Aladdin's lamp — it can draw toward you the conditions, people, and circumstances that match your conscious desires. This principle of attraction explains "coincidence" which is not accidental! When you aggressively create the object of your desire and then receptively *watch* for its manifestation, you become "tuned in" to the probabilities of other people, places, and things with corresponding needs. So, for example, when you are looking for the job you desire, you speak to everyone you know about your desire. Perhaps you have a friend who "just happened" to run into an old acquaintance who works at a place just like the one you are seeking. Or you have a hunch to pick up a newspaper that you don't usually buy, and as you turn to the classified section an ad "jumps out at you" for a position like the one you want.

There is a difference between being actively receptive and passively waiting. When you have aggressively created and formed the object of your desire, when you know it is complete, then you watch for its manifestation. You are alert, you pay attention to your environment, you see every person and place and object in your life as a potential resource, and you are ready to respond when the time is right. Knowing when to be aggressive and when to be receptive is an art. Knowing how to listen to your intuition, to give attention to the "hunches" that are inner urgings from your subconscious mind, is a skill you can develop with the practice of undivided attention and concentration. Having faith that your desire *will* manifest, there is no need to worry even when the physical results you desire have yet to come to pass. You watch, you expect, and welcome the "signs" that demonstrate your creation is in the process of coming into being. This is practicing receptivity.

Passivity, on the other hand, is leaving your life to chance which amounts to other stronger minds ruling you. When you wait to see what will happen without ever forming an object of your desire, you are being passive. When you let opportunities pass you by, saying "I guess it wasn't meant to be" you are being passive. Passivity produces victim consciousness. You find yourself being the victim of conditions and circumstances, being stepped upon by people who are bullies, or simply wasting your life waiting for things to happen to you.

Here is an example of how I used visualization to create the "perfect" job. I had just moved to Kansas City and needed employment immediately, as I had very little money saved. Because I was volunteering a great amount of time to direct a School of Metaphysics center and to teach classes, I had specific requirements for my ideal job. I hadn't decided exactly what I wanted to do on my job, but I did know what I wanted for ideal conditions. I wanted to travel no more than fifteen minutes to work, wanted to work a Monday to Friday position, thirty hours a week, wanted to earn $6 an hour, and wanted a place where I could share my discoveries about metaphysics. I also wanted to work with people who were creative, because I figured that would make my work environment stimulating.

I wrote down these conditions and also wrote down my strengths. I was responsible, dependable, intelligent, quick thinking, articulate, good typist, good with figures, able to communicate well with people. I was prompt. I started looking through the newspaper and suddenly an ad "jumped out" to capture my attention. It said, "Bearprint. Good with people. $5 an hour." I didn't know what the job entailed, and it was less money than I wanted, but something inside myself told me to call. I called, and a friendly voice answered. They told me that they had been swamped with calls and applications and were no longer setting up interviews. Immediately I projected a strong image of myself being responsible and dependable and said, "I know I have a lot of assets to offer your company. Are you willing to set up just one more interview?" The man hesitated, and said yes, if I could come over in the next fifteen minutes. He gave me directions and I jumped in my car.

I timed myself when I left the house and checked the time when I arrived at the company. Thirteen minutes. Number one condition of my ideal had been satisfied. When I walked in I discovered that this was a small printing company and from the glossy, four-color art posters on the wall I could tell that their printing jobs were for artistic, creative clients. I met the owner, who was a young, energetic man with definite ideas about service to customers. He told me that they had been having difficulty organizing their jobs and wanted a receptionist/secretary/bookkeeper who would create flow charts to trace the progress of the printing jobs and to handle the customers' calls. He was a good printer but not very effective at organization.

I described to him my background with taking care of finances for the nonprofit organization I directed, my public relations experience, and my many secretarial jobs. He introduced me to the other employees, a graphic artist who was recently out of architecture school, and two other printers. Each one had a unique talent, and the four of them coordinated their efforts to produce high quality printing for such prestigious clients as the Kansas City Ballet and Worlds of Fun, Missouri's equivalent to Disneyland. I liked the place, the sincerity of the people, the strong artistic drive that each expressed. I could tell that in working with the customers I would be in contact with the artistic circle in Kansas City. The owner seemed impressed with my skills but still had many other job applicants to consider.

During the interview, I had seen a stack of posters in the

corner that were very artistic and attractive. On closer examination I saw that it was a Bearprint calendar. The artwork was an original piece designed by a student of the Kansas City Art Institute. I thought very strongly, "I want one of those. They are beautiful." Mark, the owner, shook my hand after the interview and then said, "Would you like one of our calendars?" I said yes, I'd love one, and walked out with it in my hand.

That evening, I visualized myself going to work, driving the thirteen minutes, sitting at the desk, talking on the phone with the customers, greeting the art director of the Kansas City Ballet. I imaged myself typing out the accounts receivable receipts and organizing the desk which was a mess. I knew I could do the required job well and it fit all of my specifications except the salary.

The next day I fully expected Mark to call me and offer me the job. All day I stayed home so that I wouldn't miss the phone call, but it never came. The following night I was a little concerned, and imaged myself working at the printing place again. This time I imaged myself showing up early to work and doing extra tasks. I also reviewed the interview I had had in my mind, wondering if I had said anything to jeopardize my chances of getting the job. Then I remembered all of Mark's questions about my involvement with the School of Metaphysics. I also remembered how receptive he had been to my thought about the calendar which he offered me. So I imaged his face in my mind, and projected the thought, "I want to work for you. Your company is very prosperous and artistic and I admire the respect you have for your work. You produce high quality posters. I am responsible and I respect the choices I make. I am quick and efficient, I have good organizational skills. I am a very good employee."

The following day I called him, and Mark said, "You know, I was just thinking about you. We've narrowed down our applicants and it's between you and one other person. But I'm a little concerned about how much time you spend with the School of Metaphysics. Will this interfere with your job?" I assured him that it wouldn't and gave him a couple of job references from my former employers. Then I told him that I really wanted the job because I was impressed with the company and would like to work for them. In one hour he called back and said that they would like me to work there if I was still interested. I told him that I was, but that I had wanted to earn $6 an hour, which I told him during our initial interview. He said he'd love to pay me that but their budget couldn't afford it; would I take $5.75? I agreed, and started work the next day.

Here is another example of the use of visualization to create an ideal job. Again, I had just moved to a new city and needed a job right away. I arrived in St. Louis on Sunday night and determined that I would have a job the next day. I bought a newspaper and checked the ads, circling those that looked promising. One interview was in an office building. As I was leaving, I "just happened" to check the building's directory and saw a temporary agency listed. On a hunch, I rode the elevator up and went to apply to the agency.

The agency had a battery of tests which I took. With excellent typing skills and a large vocabulary, along with good reasoning skills, I scored high on all the tests. They were time consuming and by the time I was finished it was 4:00 p.m. As I was about to leave, the phone rang. It was a client needing a temporary employee the next day, as they had just had an employee who became sick. The woman turned to me and asked if I was ready to start work the next day. I said, "Yes!" joyfully.

I hadn't even asked what kind of company it was. I just knew it was for a clerk typist and got the directions. As I drove to the job, I saw a building with the name Times Mirror, which I recognized as a large publishing company. "Boy, wouldn't it be neat to work there," I thought, as I had previously imagined myself working for a company where I could use and develop writing and editorial skills. But I also knew that it was more important for me to work right away than to wait for the "perfect" job.

I brought my attention back to the paper on which I had written directions. Was I surprised to discover that the address I was seeking was for this Times Mirror company. When I walked in I discovered that my temporary assignment was in the Human Resources Department. I worked there for about three months, and thoroughly enjoyed the people there. They were friendly, sincere, and all liked people. Furthermore, I received much information on the world of editing and publishing and had access to every new job that was available in the company.

Amanda, who was the head of personnel, looked at my resume for no charge and gave me tips on how to rewrite it to highlight my skills with writing, proofreading, and editing. I had developed skills in all of these areas even though I had never had a formal job as an editor.

During the three-month temporary assignment, I applied for several jobs within the company for proofreader and editorial jobs. Every time I was turned down to my surprise and dismay. I wanted a job with flexible hours, a certain salary, in which I could use editorial and writing skills, and have contact with interesting people. I realized that many of the jobs for which I had been applying did not meet these conditions. Most had fairly rigid hours and involved paperwork with very little human contact.

Then, my supervisor told me that a new job was opening up in another department that was an assistant to a Developmental Editor. Unlike most of the other editorial jobs within the company, Developmental Editors worked directly with the authors and the job involved writing as well as editing. This job seemed to fit the bill. The job hadn't even been advertised yet, but my supervisor recommended I go over and talk with the woman who was going to be hiring an assistant. When I met her and heard about the job, I knew that this was it. It did involve editing, but it also involved extensive contact with authors, with different people involved in the production of the manuscripts and would give me an opportunity to do some rewriting of chapters written by foreign authors.

I told the Developmental Editor I was very interested in the job, but I needed to have hours that were flexible. "Oh, that's no problem," she said. "We have flex time in this department. As long as you work your thirty hours you can work them anytime you want, coming in as early as 6:30 a.m. and leaving as late as 7:00 p.m." After the interview, she told me that she wanted to hire me but that as a formality they still needed to advertise the job. The ad for the job appeared in the paper and ran for two weeks, but "curiously," few people applied although usually the company was flooded with applications for this type of position. I got the job.

I learned from this experience that if I had gotten a different job I would not have been available for this one, which fit all the conditions I desired. By continuing to apply for positions I learned about my desires, and with positive expectations I bided my time until the kind of position I really wanted opened up.

Balancing the aggressive and receptive principles of creation activates the most potent, enthralling, universal phenomena of nature: *love*. Think about this. Every creation involves the use of aggressive and receptive energies, from the blending of sperm and egg, to the positive and negative ions in electron bonds, to the male and female generative organs in plants. The attraction between aggressive and receptive energies is called love. When you "fall in love" you are experiencing the relationship between the aggressive and receptive qualities, and usually you desire (or at least fantasize) to produce offspring from the union. When you are creating, whether it is writing a novel or painting a picture, or developing a new business or designing a house, you experience the uplifting, inspiring, expansive quality of love. People who love their work are creative; people who create love their lives!

When you love what you do you become an attractive center. You exhibit the magnetic, compelling, drawing power called charisma. The secret of developing charisma is the ability to create a clear, solid thought-form image and broadcast it. Other minds will be drawn to the magnetic, attractive power of your clearly defined thought forms. Think about any person who has had a profound influence on large numbers of people. Whether they were a statesman, politician, religious leader, actor or actress, the common factor is that they had a presence about them, cultivated and created by the clarity of their thoughts.

It is easy to be physically active and energetic when you are inspired by love. You desire to act because you can perceive the outcome of your actions and efforts. You know they will pay off in producing the beloved object of your desire. When you expect to receive what you desire, you are effectively using the power of receptivity. Just as expectant parents prepare a nursery to receive their baby when he or she is born, as an expectant mental parent, it is important to prepare to receive the objects of your desire. Let's use the example of the job again. Suppose you are applying for a job in which you will be working in an office. Part of your preparation would be to obtain clothing appropriate for office wear. Your preparation could include the purchase of a briefcase and other items you will use in your office. Preparing for the interview itself would include researching the company so that you can intelligently answer questions and so that you have a clear idea of what the position will involve.

You will remember from the last chapter that purpose involves *who you are becoming* as you move toward your ideals. Part of your preparation for receiving the object of your desire is to imagine clearly who will you be in your new position. Have you imagined yourself being poised, businesslike, authoritative, efficient, calm, energetic? Have you imagined yourself commanding respect? Imaging the changed *you* in the changed circumstances is how you prepare yourself to *be* in the new place you desire. It is unfortunate that people do not always do this. Recently I saw a television program about people who had won millions of dollars in the lottery. In every case, within a year, the winners had not only spent their winnings, they had incurred debts so that they owed more than they had before winning the prize. This was obviously a select group but it illustrates what occurs when proper preparation has not taken place. The people who won the money may have visualized the physical object of desire (money) but they had not changed their self image from being poor (never having enough, spending beyond their means) to being wealthy (knowing how to use resources wisely). Preparation for receiving the fortune could have involved imaging how to *think* differently to handle the great influx of money.

A good way to prepare to receive success is to associate with other people who have what you want. If you want to imagine what it would be like to be a foreign diplomat, live with a family in a foreign country for six months or a year. If you are

..sidering a job in publishing, become an intern for a summer in a publishing company to try it on for size. If you are thinking about having a child, obtain a job as a live-in nanny or babysit for infants. In this way you can experience what it will be like and it will aid you to prepare for being there.

An important element in your activity is communication. The word communicate comes from a root word which means communion, to participate. When you communicate your desires you are setting up conditions for your whole mind to participate in their fulfillment. You create desires in your conscious mind, but it is in the subconscious mind that they are developed. Until you communicate your desires, how is your subconscious mind to know what you want? Your subconscious mind communicates with images, pictures; therefore, it is necessary to create a clearly defined picture image in your conscious mind and to communicate it to your subconscious mind. Affirmations may be used as a form of communication *only when* there is a mental image that accompanies the words you affirm. For example, suppose it is your desire to be wealthy. You can say and write the words, "I am wealthy. I have abundance at my command. All the resources of the universe are mine to use. I am helping others to abundance and receiving multiplied what I desire and need." When you form an image to go along with these words they will be very effective. The power of the spoken word will intensify the projection of your mental broadcast. However, if you say these words and image yourself being poor, never having enough, having to scrape to make ends meet, the words will be meaningless. Cause yourself to create strong thought-form images and describe them in the words you speak and write. Then you will be using the power of the spoken word.

Another benefit of communication is that you enable other people to participate in the fulfillment of your desire. Remember that you are always broadcasting mental images and that there are always other minds with corresponding needs. How will you know when there is another individual in your environment with a corresponding need? Through communication. Here is an example. Several years ago, I was supervising a center of metaphysics in Topeka, Kansas. The School of

Metaphysics was renting a building to hold classes and for the teachers to live, and we had a good deal with a landlord who believed in what we were doing. Since the staff was volunteer and the classes available on a donation basis, we wanted to keep our operating expenses low so that we could serve as many people as possible. The landlord sold the building, and the new landlord tripled the rent! Needless to say, we decided to move, and we had thirty days to find a new place. Cheryl, the director of the center, created a clear image of the kind of house she wanted to rent to use for the classes. She decided she wanted a house with four bedrooms, two bathrooms, plenty of parking, easily accessible from the highway, a large room for holding lectures and seminars, good-sized kitchen, and she wanted to pay the same rent we had been paying: $350 per month. She wrote down this ideal image and communicated it to all of her students. One of them, an artist, even drew a picture of the kind of house we wanted. Then Cheryl proceeded to invest her time in the physical activity of looking for a place, checking the newspaper ads, going to look at houses, talking with everyone she knew about what we were seeking. The days passed and we hadn't found what we wanted. Every house she looked at was a little bit closer, but each one had some drawback: one only had one bathroom, one had very little parking, one had a tiny kitchen, another was perfect but the price was too high. The days were moving quickly and we had to find a place by the end of the month. Cheryl kept looking, kept talking, kept putting out the word to her students about what we wanted. Then, with only five days left, she started packing up the school's belongings to prepare to move, even though we had not yet signed a lease on a new place. Finally, the Saturday before the last day of the month (which was Monday) we settled on a house. It was close to the desired ideal, but didn't fit all the conditions. It had four bedrooms, two baths, a good-sized living room to use for lectures, but the kitchen was kind of small, and the parking was not really adequate. Plus, the rent was $400, close to our ideal but a little bit higher than what we wanted. Well, we figured that we had to deal with the conditions as they stood, and with only two days left we would sign a lease. We agreed to meet the landlord at 9:00 a.m. Monday to sign the lease on this house.

Saturday night at 7:00 p.m. Cheryl received a phone call from one of her students. She had been looking in the paper that day and saw a little ad which read, "HOUSE FOR RENT. MAKE YOUR OWN DEAL." There was a phone number and that was it. Cheryl got excited and called the number. No answer. She called again an hour later, still no answer. Meanwhile she and all of her students were packing up books, kitchen supplies, towels, all of the school's belongings so that we'd be ready to move on Monday. Cheryl kept calling the number from this ad but still received no answer. She called Sunday all day — and still there was no answer at that number. Monday morning came. Remember, we were supposed to sign a lease on the other house at 9:00 a.m. Cheryl started calling the number in the paper at 7:00 a.m. No answer. 7:30 — no answer. Finally, at 8:00 a woman answered the phone. She was a receptionist at a dentist's office. The dentist was the landlord of the house and was scheduled to be in the office at 9:00. The receptionist said to call back then. Cheryl explained the situation, and said she had to reach him before 9:00 because we had another appointment. The receptionist said that was impossible. Cheryl, anxious to see this place, said, "You don't understand! I am a teacher of mind, I dedicate my life to helping people, we need a place to hold our classes. I just have to talk to him!" The receptionist, believing in Cheryl's sincerity, gave her the dentist's home number. Cheryl called and arranged to meet him at the house at 8:30, half an hour before the scheduled time to sign the lease on the other place.

When we arrived at this house, Cheryl and I drew in our breath. It was very accessible from the highway, easy to find, and just down the street from the VA Hospital — a well-known landmark. Although the house was on a busy street known to everyone, it had off-street parking to accommodate about twenty cars. When we walked in to the living room, we were struck by its size — large enough to hold twenty-five or thirty people. The house had five bedrooms, two bathrooms plus a shower in the basement, a full attic and full basement. It was even larger than what Cheryl had visualized and would easily accommodate our needs. I noticed that the place was sturdy, but had obviously not been taken care of by the previous tenants. When they moved, they left garbage in the rooms, and they had painted the walls very strange colors: electric blue, hot pink. I asked the landlord what they had been paying and he said $650 per month. I asked why they left and he said that they had not been paying their utility bills and the utility company shut off the electricity and then came to the door demanding payment. They just disappeared in the middle of the night. From collecting this information, it became apparent that he was looking for tenants who would be responsible. He even said so, saying that he was not a landlord by trade, he was a dentist, and what he wanted were tenants he could count on to pay rent and take care of the place and not give him a hassle. I knew that we were responsible and could supply good references. I asked him what he wanted for rent, and he said, what do you want to pay? I said, $275, thinking that would give us some bargaining room and that we could probably pay the $350 we had wanted. He didn't even hesitate when I offered $275 and said, great, that would be fine!

So through communication Cheryl was able to have not only what she desired, but benefits she hadn't even included in her picture. Because her student knew what she wanted, she participated in fulfilling the desire, because the landlord communicated his needs we knew we had what would correspond to his needs (responsible people), because we communicated our needs to him he was willing to cooperate with us. Everyone got what they wanted!

Speaking your desires out loud will aid you to create them much more quickly. It will also aid you to identify when you are limiting your imagination. The words that tumble out of your mouth describe the images in your mind, even when you are unaware of those images. Practice listening to yourself. You can become self-aware by hearing your own words, hearing the thoughts they describe, and creating the thoughts that will produce the successes you desire.

Treasure Maps

When you go on vacation, you plan your route, decide which roads to take, and therefore know which direction to go. In creating your life, you can also make a map to guide you to your destination. Since the end result is the desire you want to fulfill, we call it a treasure map.

We have said that the mind communicates with pictures. In making a treasure map, you will be using pictures to plan the steps to your goal. Start with a goal that you want to reach within thirty days. Thirty days is a short enough period of time for you to see results and watch your progress. It is long enough to give you time to plan and to create your goal.

Once you have decided upon a thirty-day goal, find some old magazines to cut up. Look through the magazines to find a picture to represent your end goal. Then find other pictures to represent one day of activity toward your goal. Your map will have thirty pictures on it, one for each day. The final picture will be your goal. Post this map on a wall where you can see it every day. Every day look at the picture and visualize yourself going through the activity to attain your goal. You can even cross off the pictures day by day as you accomplish them. You will find that this step-by-step map will help you to visualize the "how to" and will therefore aid you in developing will power.

The first time I used a treasure map I decided I wanted to stretch my imagination a bit. I had used a What I Want in Life list with success, but there was one goal that I was having a little difficulty believing. This goal was a new place to live. At the time, my residence was Ann Arbor, Michigan. Ann Arbor is a college town and at that time the vacancy rate was the lowest in the country. In other words, it was a landlord's paradise. Places to rent were very expensive and often low quality. Landlords knew that there were more people looking for places to live than there were places available, so they could charge exorbitant rents for slums.

I had been living in a house with six roommates. It had become crowded and I wanted to live in a respectable place rather than a thrown-together college crash pad. Because the living conditions in Ann Arbor were so crowded, I had stayed in that house. After practicing visualization for awhile I had begun to believe that I could create conditions I desired in my life rather than accepting limitations. But this idea of finding a nice place for a low amount of money... I had difficulty believing it. When I was presented with the idea of a treasure map, I figured I'd test it out. I decided to use as a goal the kind of house I wanted to live in.

If I'm really going to test this, I thought, I might as well put into my image *all* the conditions I desire. I decided I wanted to live in a comfortable, respectable house that was on a quiet street, set back from the road. I wanted a garden, a fireplace, and a piano. And I wanted to pay $125 a month rent. When I talked to my friends about this, they said, "Laurel, you're crazy! There is no place like that for such a low rent in Ann Arbor." I decided then that I would prove it to them. Their doubts challenged me to prove to myself the value of what I was studying about mind!

So I set to work to make a map. First, I found a picture of a warm living room, with a fire blazing in the fireplace, a piano in the corner. I found a picture of a garden which I set right outside the living room window. And I imaged myself playing the piano in the living room with the fire crackling.

Then I found pictures for the steps of activity I'd take. I imaged myself checking the newspaper, looking at the bulletin boards in the Student Activities Center, talking to people, reading my What I Want in Life list, riding my bicycle to look at houses. I found thirty pictures to represent thirty days of such activity. I drew a couple of the pictures when I didn't find a magazine picture to match what I had in mind. I posted my treasure map on my bedroom wall and looked at it every morning, then I proceeded to take the activity represented by that day.

On the tenth day, I rode to the Student Activities Center to read the bulletin board in the Housing Office. I had done this a couple of times before. On this day, I saw a notice that I hadn't seen before: "Professor going on sabbatical. House for rent for responsible adults." I wrote down the phone number and called as soon as I got back home. A friendly woman answered the phone and said that she lived alone in a three-bedroom house. She was taking a sabbatical leave for a year and had a furnished house she wanted taken care of. She gave me the address and I hopped on my bicycle to go check it out. As I rode up the street, I marveled at the huge trees that lined both sides. There were beautiful old mansions on this block. I looked for the number of the house and couldn't find it. After I had ridden up and down twice, I finally spotted a trellis with vines growing on it between two huge houses. A house number was on the trellis —the address I was seeking. I walked up the walk, a stone walk that led to a clearing behind the vine-covered trellis. There, set back from the road, was a quaint stone house that looked as if it belonged in a fairy tale. Surrounding the house was a well-tended flower garden and to the side was a sizeable vegetable garden. (In my treasure map I had only visualized one garden!) I rang the bell, and the woman who greeted me led me into the kitchen. She had some hot chocolate on the stove and offered me some. Then she led me into the living room. It was small, lined with book cases, and in the corner was a baby grand piano. On one wall was a stone fireplace and I could tell from the ashes that it was well used. She showed me around the house, led me upstairs to the three bedrooms.

I could scarcely contain my enthusiasm. This house was exactly what I had pictured! I asked her what the rent was, and she said $400. With a quick calculation, I could tell that with two roommates each of us would pay $133 for our own bedroom. I immediately said, I'll take it. She was pleased, as I was responsible and she knew that from my references. I was pleased, because this little house had every feature I'd imagined, with one exception. The rent was slightly higher than I'd wanted. But I realized that I had doubted that one element of my picture. I didn't fully believe that I could find what I wanted for

$125. What I know now from further experience, and didn't know then, is that I could have asked her if she would have been willing to rent the house to us for $375, which would have made the rent $125 apiece for my roommates and me. And if I had visualized that idea strongly, she probably would have said yes, since we were the kind of responsible adults she was seeking. But even so, at $133 a month, this house was a wonderful deal and provided a wonderful living experience.

You can use treasure maps for any goal you desire. Many people use this tool when they are dieting or have goals for physical fitness. This thirty-day plan lends itself well to such goals, because it is simple to break down into daily steps the plan that will lead to the final result. For example, if your goal is to lose five pounds in thirty days, you might have a picture of a physically fit, toned person as your final image and you can even superimpose a photo of your own face on the desirable body picture. You could choose images of healthy foods, drinking water, walking, swimming or other exercise, and so forth. Each image gives you a step of activity that will produce the result you desire. In my case, I didn't even need to use the map for the entire thirty days, as I manifested my desired result in ten. You may find that, too.

The treasure map will help you envision your desired accomplishment. As with any visualization, you will want to prepare yourself to receive the object of your desire. I learned this the hard way. One of the first items I created using this tool was a car. This was a "big" desire for me, one that in the beginning was a little difficult for me to imagine and believe. There were reasons I had difficulty imagining myself driving a car—I failed a road test when I was first applying for a driver's license, and since that time I had been afraid to drive although I had finally gotten a license. To compound the "problem," I received my license in New York where the highways were tremendously congested and traffic conditions are hazardous. Although I received a license at the age of sixteen, I had never owned a car, and by the time I was twenty-two I had never practiced driving. I was embarrassed to admit that I was afraid to drive, and the more I suppressed my fear, the greater it loomed in my imagination.

I finally decided it was time for me to grow up and to own my own car, for I recognized that I was dependent on other people to drive me around. Although I used the bus and bicycle for most of my activities, I was expanding my desires and wanted to travel greater distances which required a car. The car was my ideal, and the purpose I created for it was to learn how to be responsible and mature. The only problem was that I didn't envision myself being responsible with the car. I imaged myself being afraid and unprepared to use it fully. Nevertheless, I was determined to break through this fear and I put on my map the kind of car I wanted—a Volkswagen. I found pictures from magazines to portray the steps of activity — working, saving the money, looking in the newspaper, talking to friends, looking at cars, etc. I test drove several cars and none of them fit my image. On the twenty-third day, I spoke with a friend who had a mechanic friend whose wife was selling her car, a green Volkswagen Superbeetle. My friend took me to look at the car, which was in excellent condition and had been well taken care of since the owner's husband was a mechanic. It had brand new tires and the price I wanted to pay. I bought the car.

This could be the end of the story, but it was just the beginning. I wanted to be independent, and my own car would give me the freedom to make my own choices about where to go and when to go there. But I had not learned about how to take care of a vehicle, nor had I changed my image of myself to include being free and responsible and mature. The first change to which I needed to respond was to admit that there were basic facts of life I had never learned—like how to pump gas. Because I had not driven, I had never learned this. I was embarrassed to ask anyone to show me, because I thought that I ought to know this at the age of twenty-two. A friend of mine borrowed my "new" car the second day I had it to go grocery shopping. I told her with relief that she could borrow it if she would put some gas in it and gave her $5 to fill the tank. (This was my way out of having to learn a skill I thought I should already know.) Amy returned the car to me, handed me the $5 and said she didn't have time to get the gas. I was panicked, because I had to drive someone to the airport the next day and was worried about having enough gas in the car. "Oh, don't worry," said Amy, "Volkswagens hardly use any gas at all. You'll have enough." I took her word for it.

The next day I drove my friend to the airport. It was my first time driving on a highway, and I was a little scared on the return trip since I was alone in the car, but I was also exhilarated at the new-found freedom of having my own vehicle. Suddenly, the car started slowing down. I was in the middle lane on a Detroit highway that was crowded with cars, and I began to panic. I had just gotten the car and had no idea what was wrong. I hadn't even discovered yet where the hazard light button was located. I had been studying metaphysics for a few months and all at once the words from one of my lessons sounded loudly in my mind: "Thought directed with intelligence is the most powerful force in the universe." *Immediately* I began to visualize the cars behind me going around me, because I knew that if I let my fear take over and imagined them crashing into me, that would occur. Miraculously, the cars went around me.

The car kept slowing down, and I still couldn't figure out what was wrong. I knew that I didn't have much time, and I started to steer the car to the right to get on the shoulder, but before I could get it all the way on the shoulder it just stopped, right in the middle of the highway. I breathed deeply to calm my racing heart and visualized someone coming over to push the car to the side of the road. In less than a minute, two cars pulled over and two men came over and pushed the lightweight Volkswagen onto the shoulder out of the way of the traffic. One of the men kindly drove me to the nearest exit, at which there was a gas station with a tow truck. The tow truck came and towed my car. I told them I didn't know what was wrong with it. To my embarrassment and also relief, the mechanic discovered that the only problem with my car was that it was out of gas. It was not a mechanical failure, as I had feared. He showed me how to pump my own gas, I paid him for his time, and drove on my way, with a red face and renewed determination to learn responsibility!

The experience was a productive one for me because it showed me how powerful my mind was. I learned how to create the physical object I desired, the car, and I also learned how to avoid danger by visualizing the cars going around me. I envisioned help, and help arrived in a split second. And I also learned that my desire to build the qualities I wanted—maturity, responsibility, confidence—manifested quickly as well. The *thing* did not give me those qualities. Although I was embarrassed to admit that I had not already built the qualities I desired, I quickly changed my thought to image myself having and exhibiting and expressing what I wanted to be. I gave myself a gift in this experience—the permission to learn and grow, even as an adult. This has been of tremendous benefit to me to this day.

Here is another example of how a treasure map aided me to create rather quickly a desire that had taken awhile to manifest. I was living in Colorado and teaching people how to teach classes in metaphysics. For some time, one of the centers in which I was teaching was having difficulty drawing in new people to the classes. I decided that I wanted to have a lot of people to teach, because I love the lessons and loved the changes I had seen people make through their studies. Having used treasures maps before, I knew that this tool would work to create the class I desired to teach.

I started looking through magazines and catalogs, and found pictures of people who were smiling. I found pictures of people who were talking to one another — in the office, on the beach, in a restaurant, on the street. I cut out pictures of people in groups of two and three, singly, in groups of five and ten. I arranged the pictures of people on a poster board, including any scenes I had found of people talking to one another. I also put words on this map, and as I cut out the words I envisioned people talking to each other. "Share what you are learning." "Talk to each other." "Share what you know with the world." "Love your friends—tell them what you know." These were some of the words on the treasure map that accompanied the pictures of people conversing with each other. There was one place on the map where I glued pictures of individuals in groups of two and three, combining them to form a larger group of sixteen. This was the ideal size of an intimate class in applied metaphysics.

After I had created the map, I posted it on the wall of the

school and spoke with all of the students about visualizing every day the image of what they had learned and sharing it with others. "Talk to people," I told them. "Share what you are learning." I also set up some lectures on different metaphysical topics and called people who had expressed interest in classes. The night of the registration, the new students introduced themselves. I had taught a lot of metaphysics classes, but this was the first one in which so many of the new people had come from someone personally telling them about it. One woman came with her sister. Michelle, the first woman, had heard about the class from her boyfriend, whose roommate was a student in the school. She brought her sister with her. Another person, Mary, came because a friend of hers had seen an ad in the paper. The friend never showed up, but Mary came from her friend's word-of-mouth contact. Roger heard about the class from his ex-wife who had found out about the school when she passed it on the way to a yard sale. John came because his sister who was a student at a different center had told him about it and he discovered there was a school close to where he lived, in a different city from his sister. And so on. The class was composed of sixteen people, exactly the number of the group on the map. Furthermore, there were the same number of men and women as in the picture on the map! The class was an exact reproduction of the image on the map, and the people had come in the ways described on the map.

This example was very dramatic because I had imaged the exact activity and this produced exact results. In the following example, I used a treasure map to visualize the desired results, but I was not as specific about the means to fulfill the desire. I was expectant and willing to respond, and this caused the map to be successful. My desire was for a typewriter—to be exact, an IBM Selectric typewriter. I wanted to pay $25 or less for the typewriter, even though used IBM Selectrics usually sell for $150 or more. They are excellent machines and will last a long time when they are cared for. I found a picture of a typewriter from an old office supply catalog and put this as the desired goal. Then I found pictures to represent the steps of activity—calling office supply places, visiting an IBM manufacturer to check on the possibility of receiving a donation, calling schools to find out about purchasing used equipment.

At the time I made this map I was working in the office of a publishing company. I used a typewriter and so did the other people in my office. The company had hundreds of employees, most of whom had typewriters. One day, I noticed that there was an old typewriter sitting unused on the floor of our supply room. I asked my supervisor if the company ever donated old typewriters and explained that I was a teacher at the School of Metaphysics and was looking for a typewriter for our use. She told me that the company did not make donations, but that they did hold an auction twice a year to sell outdated equipment. The next auction was coming up in a couple of weeks. I found out the procedure for the auction. Each employee in the company was eligible to participate. The items for auction were displayed in the back storeroom, and employees could bid by writing their bids in a sealed envelope and submitting them. After all the bids were submitted, the highest one would receive the item.

I looked at the items in the auction, and lo and behold, there were four IBM Selectric typewriters. I submitted bids for each one, bidding $25 apiece. The day the bids were opened, I was disappointed to find out that my bids were lower than the others submitted and all four had been sold to other employees. Nevertheless, I kept visualizing my goal and called around to find other places that would have the typewriter I wanted. A few days later, I got a call from the manager of the auction who told me that the person who had bid higher than me did not want the typewriter after all, as it needed repair. He asked me if I still wanted to pay $25 for it. I decided to get it, even though it needed repair, because I had not had any success finding an IBM Selectric anywhere else. When I went to pick up the typewriter, the manager told me that another employee had declined the typewriter they bid on because it needed repair as well, and he gave me both typewriters for $25. Now I had two IBM Selectric typewriters for $25, but I was faced with the repair.

One of my co-workers told me that there was a man who came once a month to repair and clean the IBM typewriters the company used. She suggested I talk to him and that he could probably repair the typewriters for a small fee. The next time he was visiting the office, I asked him about the typewriters I had purchased. He volunteered to look at them and when he discovered all they needed was basic cleaning, he cleaned them for no charge. The typewriters were not broken, they had just gotten gummed up from sitting unused and uncovered and with a little cleaning they were fine. So with the aid of a treasure map, creative use of resources, and help from friends, I manifested two IBM Selectric typewriters in good working order for only $25.

This story points out an important element to remember in your visualizing work: looking for resources and responding to them once you have found them. There were two people who passed up perfectly good typewriters because they didn't want to bother taking the next step to find out what it would require to repair them. There were hundreds of people in the company who never even came to the warehouse to investigate the auction because they were too busy. Several of my co-workers had expressed an interest in the auction, but when the day came they didn't want to spend their lunch hour or break time to wander around a dirty warehouse. As a result they missed out on some excellent bargains.

When you create complete, detailed images you are willing to put forth some effort to respond to resources in your environment, for you know that your efforts will pay off! This causes you to look at everything in your world as a possible "boon," an experience to make you one of those lucky people who always seem to get their way.

Affirmations II

As you practice using creative imagery in your life, you will discover a growing awareness of your own power, strength, and vitality. You will find that you can have anything you desire and become anyone you imagine! Sometimes you will find that your life seems miraculous because visualization is so effective for creating what you want. I have heard people who are just learning to visualize say that it is scary to find out about the power of their own minds. Learning the mechanics of the mind helps to change this fear to curiosity, for as you master the knowledge you can wield its power responsibly and carefully. Any time that you want to strengthen your resolve or become more centered and focused with your creative imagery, you can use affirmations. They will help you to become more secure, definite, and clear. If you tend to be influenced by other people's thoughts, affirmations are tremendously helpful when you are surrounded by negative-thinking people. Your own affirmations will keep you focused on the thought-form images you want. I have already presented affirmations that will aid you to image yourself as an abundant, productive, happy person. Now you will begin to understand how and why these affirmations work.

Affirmations help you to concentrate on the object of your desire. I have seen many books that recommend writing affirmations and posting them on mirrors, car dashboards, refrigerators, notebooks — anywhere you are likely to see them — to read and say every day. "I am a child of God." "Abundance and prosperity are mine." "I am slim and fit and full of energy." And so on! These affirmations will work *only when* they are said with an accompanying visualized thought-form image. The language of the mind is images, not words. Your subconscious mind receives images which you form in your conscious mind.

The words are used to describe the images you create in your mind. Thus, when you say, "I am slim and fit and full of energy," and you picture yourself being slim with toned muscles, moving gracefully and quickly, being flexible and supple, feeling the tight muscles and energetic surge as you move, this affirmation will be powerful and effective. However, if you say the words but image yourself being heavy and sluggish, the words will have no effect. This is why there are some people who can diet forever or who go to the health club regularly, but remain fat and awkward. They continue to image themselves being overweight or clumsy and oftentimes they affirm this state with words like, "I'll never lose this weight," or "No matter how much I exercise, I still look like an elephant."

Use affirmations to describe in words the clearly defined thought-form images you create in your mind. Use affirmations to help you clarify your pictures. If you find yourself saying or thinking, "I know what I mean, I just can't describe it," think again! Most likely, you have a vague idea. Strive to image your thought, and this will help you to draw forth from within yourself the complete idea you want to express. In order for your subconscious mind to fulfill your desires, it needs a clearly defined thought form. If you cannot describe it in words, you have not defined it clearly. Use verbal communication to help you complete your images, so that you can describe with all your senses what your desire will look, smell, feel, taste, and sound like. When you have difficulty doing this, try reading poetry or novels to aid you. Excellent novelists are very descriptive. They will stimulate your awareness of how to use words to describe sensory detail, how to observe and record complete images.

You might consider your subconscious mind to be like the magic genie who appears in fairly tales. Anything a person wishes for they receive, whether they want it or not! Your subconscious mind does not discriminate; your conscious mind performs this important function. Therefore, you must decide what you want and image a positive picture of your desire as you say the accompanying words. "I will quit smoking. I am a non-smoker" are words people try to use to change a habit. But these words will not produce the desired result, because the image that goes along with them is smoking! It is like the "No Smoking" signs that appear in many public places — a cigarette with a red line through it. The smoker who wants to quit continues to image scenes of smoking even though he or she wants to cancel these thoughts. Your subconscious mind receives the image of the undesirable behavior — the smoking. Instead, it is more productive to say and image a positive desire. For example, "I am the master of my mind and body," along with the image of being directed, calm, and focused. When the urge to smoke affects the person wanting to change, he or she can say these words and image themselves in the new way. They are concentrating and affirming the desired thought-form image.

Affirmations that work are those which offer to the subconscious mind a positive, clear, complete and detailed image. When many senses are involved in forming the picture, it is stronger and more effective. The affirmations which follow are the same ones presented to you in Chapter 8. This time, along with each affirmation is an image you can use as you say the words. Practice this, and soon you will be able to form your own images which are personal to you and which will communicate powerfully to your subconscious mind your sincere devotion to change and growth.

I am happy, creative, and fulfilled. Picture yourself with a smile on your face, involved in your favorite creative activity, whether it be writing, painting, dancing, athletics, business, or parenting. Feel the exuberance and energy.

Life is full of unlimited resources. Picture yourself surrounded by people who are reaching out a hand to help you. Image many doors, waiting for you to open them, expecting to find money, people, or whatever you desire behind the doors.

Wherever I am, good things happen. Picture yourself walking into a room, imaging a brilliant light emanating from within you and all around you. See your light touching everyone in the room and see each person's light becoming brighter as yours contacts theirs.

I am full of joy. Picture yourself feeling light, a tingle energizing your body, smiling, hugging each person you meet.

I give thanks for the treasures in my life. Image the different areas of your life — work, school, home, and picture everything valuable in each situation. Picture yourself bowing reverently with gratitude to each person in the image.

It is a wonderful day! Picture the sky, trees, buildings, activities in your life--the interesting and varied people you will meet. Image yourself moving from one activity to the next, feeling energetic, alive, full of light, and smiling.

I love my life. Use some of the same images from the previous affirmation, and picture yourself hugging each person in the picture, visualizing a brilliant light coming from your solar plexus area and emanating throughout the whole scene, radiating the entire image with light.

I give thanks for abundance and prosperity. Image your wallet stuffed with $100 bills, your home filled with every beautiful thing you want, a garden overflowing with fruits and vegetables ready to be picked, loving people in your house, and see yourself welcoming them with open arms.

I look for the gift in every experience. Image yourself with a look of delighted surprise on your face, feeling the exhilaration and wonder of something great happening. Picture different areas of your life — your home, family, school, work — and see a wrapped present there, waiting for you to open it.

I am ready and willing to receive life's abundance. Picture yourself standing with your palms upward or with your arms outstretched as if you are about to receive a big hug from someone you love.

I love the divinity in each person I meet. Picture a person with a glowing light in their solar plexus area that radiates throughout their body. Image yourself as a brilliant creature of light in the same way, reaching out to enfold the other person in a warm embrace of light.

I salute the divinity within you. Picture yourself walking up to someone you have never met before, perceiving the warm glow of light that emanates from their solar plexus area. Image yourself reaching out your hand which is also glowing with light to touch the light in their solar plexus.

I improve the earth plane wherever I go. Picture yourself walking on a sidewalk, picking up a piece of paper that is on the ground. See yourself in a group of people and as you smile and converse, their faces begin smiling, they open their arms and are happier. You can even picture having a wand that you wave and image different scenes which become brighter and lighter as you touch them (like turning a black-and-white television scene into full color.)

I am a fountain of joy. Picture yourself as a water fountain, bubbling up and over. Feel the lightness and tingle of energy, smile, and image other people smiling and laughing as you come into contact with them.

I give ever-increasing riches from the source of my abundance. Picture yourself with paper money or gold coins, handing them to people you meet. Image yourself with an individual person or group of people, speaking truth to them, seeing their faces light up with recognition and relief.

I am a spark of light. Picture yourself with a warm glow in the center of your being. Image it growing, first small like a candle flame, then increasing in size to the size of a flashlight beam, then growing to fill your entire body with light, then radiating out beyond your body until your entire being is a silhouette of light. Image yourself walking through your experiences like this, and see your light sparking a glow of light in each person you encounter.

I am loving and generous. Picture yourself walking up to people and hugging them warmly. Image yourself speaking words of truth and giving money or food or clothes or any other valuable objects.

I am a positive influence on everything and everyone around me. Picture yourself walking into a room full of people and enfolding them with your light. Image yourself feeling calm and centered, directed and full of peace.

I bring light to every situation. Picture yourself carrying a candle with a strong, steady flame. Image yourself coming into a dark room and lighting candles along the wall, lighting candles people are holding, building a blazing bonfire in the center until the entire room is full of light and the faces of the people are bathed in light.

Every person I meet has a gift to offer. Picture yourself walking up to a stranger who is holding a wrapped present in their hands. Feel the butterflies in your stomach, the eager curiosity to find out what this person has to give you.

I have integrity, dignity, and strength. Image yourself walking tall, with a straight back, your head held high. Feel the calm center of your being, as if there were a warm glow or a steady, calm pool of water which provides nourishing peace.

I am a creative, interesting person. Picture yourself talking with people, keeping them enthralled, wearing interesting clothes, performing any creative endeavor you choose such as sculpting, weaving, dancing, cooking, singing, or writing.

I am secure and at peace. Picture yourself in a temple, with candles glowing around you or out in the woods surrounded by nature. Feel connected with a source of power within yourself. Image stillness, like a pool of water that is completely calm with complete silence.

I love and am loved. Picture yourself reaching out a hand to touch someone on the shoulder. Image yourself radiating light and enfolding another person with light. Feel a sense of connectedness with something solid within yourself. Speak truth, warmly and directly.

Today is full of hope. Picture the sun rising over the edge of a mountain. Image the muted colors of pink, peach, rose, and threads of blue. Then watch the colors become more strong and brilliant as the sun rises, illuminating the colors of the mountain, seeing the rich hues of greens and browns. Feel the energy, the exhilaration and the stillness.

I am intelligent and creative. Picture yourself in a situation you encounter daily — perhaps in a conference room at work. Image yourself concentrating, listening, and receiving information. Image a light coming on in your mind — a spark of recognition, or a sense of things "clicking" as you think and respond quickly. Picture yourself communicating with a sense of certainty about your ideas.

I am strong mentally and physically. Picture yourself lifting weights, climbing a mountain, running or walking swiftly. Image yourself easily moving, directing your attention, feeling calm and centered.

I love the people around me. Picture yourself smiling, embracing the people in your life, kissing them on the cheek, saying kind things, enfolding them with light that emanates from within and around you.

I am confident and at ease in all situations. Picture yourself walking into a room full of strangers, or on stage before a large audience, smiling, speaking truth from your experience, easily initiating the communication, feeling a sense of peace and stillness.

Every situation brings me opportunities to discover more of my power, creativity, skill and talent. Image yourself in a particular situation that is a part of your life. For example, if you are a teacher, picture yourself in the classroom teaching a lesson and experiencing the thought and feeling, "aha!" as you discover a truth you never knew before.

There are sources of support around and within me. Picture yourself with a place within your solar plexus that is steady and secure, a warm glow, soft like a kitten's fur, solid like brass. Image your light radiating from the center of your being and connecting with lights at the center of other people, forming a steady stream of light that is strong and flexible.

All things are possible. Image a map with an "X" at the center that says "You are here." Picture roads extending outward from the center, some straight, some winding, each one leading to a destination. Picture from each destination more roads extending in many different directions. If, as you imagine this, you come upon road blocks, image a road that goes around the road block. Or picture outer space, going out beyond the planets and stars and galaxies, continuing to image an infinite expanse of space.

These images are a place to start, to stimulate your own imagination. The most effective affirmations are those which emanate from you. Choose images that resonate within your being, that come alive as you picture them. Sound your words out loud, speaking them firmly and with conviction. Write them in your own handwriting and read them, being sure to create a clear image each time you do. Every time you create the image, you add life, energy, and motion to your visualized thought form, ensuring its manifestation in your life.

PART III
Your Highest Ideals

*"If one advances confidently in the direction of his dreams, and
endeavors to live the life which he has imagined,
he will meet with a success unexpected in common hours.
He will...pass an invisible boundary; new, universal,
and more liberal laws will begin to establish themselves
around and within him;
...and he will live with the license of a higher order of beings.
In proportion as he simplifies his life,
the laws of the universe will appear less complex...
If you have built castles in the air, your work need not be lost;
that is where they should be. Now put the foundations under
them....such is the character of that morrow
which mere lapse of time can never make to dawn."*
—*Henry David Thoreau*

Man As Creator

Fairy tales, mythology, classic literature and history are
filled with stories of miracles. Aladdin had a magic genie whose
sole duty and purpose was to fulfill Aladdin's desires. King
Midas received his wish to have everything he touched turn to
gold. Hercules enountered many challenges and prevailed to
win his desired rewards. Most children believe that when they
throw a coin in a wishing well, blow out the candles on a birthday
cake, ask Santa Claus or wish upon a star, their desires will be
granted. All you have to do is decide what you want and your
mind will work in magical and mysterious ways to give it to you.
Your mind has the power to say to you, "Your wish is my
command!"

Life can be an exciting adventure, a stimulating schoolroom, a world of experience which gives us opportunities to
learn, to create, and to prosper mentally, emotionally, materi-
ally, and spiritually. Every day we can awaken to the promise
of enhanced awareness. How we create our life experiences and
our world around us is determined by the degree of awareness we
possess. The more we understand the purpose for life, the more
enriched our everyday existence can be. The more we create the
situations and circumstances we desire, the more we command
the peace, contentment and happiness we deserve.

Years ago, when I was a young child of about five or six years old, I had a vision of the world as I imagined it could be. It didn't make sense to me that people were unhappy. It didn't make sense to me that people were mean, that they robbed or killed or hurt other people. I believed if people were truly doing what they wanted to do, then everyone would live in harmony and would be happy. I believed the source of such destructive actions was the unhappiness people experienced when they were living a life other than that which they desired. I thought that if someone was not doing what he or she wanted to do, he or she would take it out on other people by being nasty. My vision was that each person knew him or herself. Everyone had a "calling," a vocation which was an expression of their true, inner heart's desire. As a result, everyone was content, and everyone reached out to give to one another. Because each person had his or her own unique talents and abilities, he or she was able to help other people who didn't have those abilities. The world was like a big puzzle, and each piece was a person who was fulfilling his or her heart's desires and creating from the depth of his or her being.

Although I have matured since that time, I still believe when an individual is doing what he or she truly desires to do, when he is creating from the source of his being, he is content. I have heard objections to this idea: "You're crazy! If everyone is running around doing whatever they please there will be chaos! People will kill one another! They will damage each other's property!" I have found this to be untrue. When someone creates, he fills his soul with awareness and under-standing. If his creation benefits his soul, spiritual Self, or inner Self, it will benefit other people as well. People only hurt one another when they are denying their creative urge.

The lives of famous people illustrate this. Today we often take for granted the achievements of men and women who came before us. A person we call a "genius" is often one with a drive to pursue excellence. When one responds to the urge to reach within the depths of themselves and bring forth what they believe and know to be true, they are motivated by the highest passion. The people we remember are ones who gave themselves to life, who were always striving to reach higher, to delve deeper, to demand of themselves the best. Our lives are different because such people give; their influence spans generations.

Consider Shakespeare, whose understanding of universal truth and the nature of humanity has been passed down for centuries from the words of his pen. Or Euclid, who defined structure, and whose postulates and axioms form the basis of today's geometry although he lived in 300 B.C. Albert Einstein is another example of an individual whose creativity has influenced the entire world. Although he never did well in school, his curiosity about the universe led him to discover the principle of relativity and eventually the tremendous power of atomic reactions. Einstein believed in a God "who reveals himself in the harmony of all being" and his scientific research is a testimony to his drive to discover and know his own Creator.

Marie Curie, another scientist, overcame obstacles to bring the discovery of radioactivity to the world. Born in Poland during a time when education was forbidden to women, Curie travelled to France to attend the Sorbonne, and graduated first in her class with concentration in physics and mathematics, unheard of for women at the time. Her original intention was to become educated to teach so that she could bring about her vision of a free Poland. Her scientific discoveries led her down a different path, and through her dedication, research, and inquisitive thinking, we now have radiation therapy and a greater understanding of the structure of the atom. Thomas Jefferson had a similar dedication to education. Of his many achievements he considers the establishment of the University of Virginia to be his greatest. Jefferson was committed to a vision of insuring that each person be free to live up to the potential given to us by our Creator. The primary author of the Declaration of Independence, Jefferson believed that "the God who gave us life gave us liberty" and through his actions ensured that the United States of America would provide a structure to enable its citizens to live this truth.

Leonardo da Vinci was another individual who was so full of talents he excelled in many diverse areas. An artist and sculptor, civil engineer, architect, military planner, inventor, scientist, and draftsman, in all of his activities he held a vision of a better life. He drew designs for a flying machine, the mechanics of which are used in aircraft today. Dissecting corpses and using his artistic genius, he drew the first anatomy textbook with accurate pictures of the human body. His ideas were so far ahead of their time that many were not made into machines during his day, but nonetheless he gave what he knew and had the courage to explore ideas that seemed crazy to those less enlightened than he.

There are many stories of men and women like these whose lives continue to touch ours generations later. These people have changed the world through their incessant search for truth, their drive and determination to find answers to the meaning of life, and their use of imagination, will power, and mental discipline. They were not born this way, they became this way through living lives of purpose and through keeping alive the inner voice of truth. The great American philosopher and writer Ralph Waldo Emerson said, "To believe your own thought, to believe that what is true for you in your private heart is true for all men, — that is genius." When a person discovers a truth that has universal application and has the courage to communicate these ideas to the world, he or she makes a mark. Humanity progresses as a result of their desire and willingness to create a better world.

We each have an urge to create. We are happy when we are creating. Look at children. They are always inventing stories, designing clubs with rules and regulations of order, building houses with blocks, drawing, making up songs. Unfortunately, gradually and subtly children learn to squelch their creative drive. Adults tell them they need to be serious, to be practical. They hear in verbal and nonverbal ways, "You will never amount to anything. You're too idealistic! Don't expect too much and you won't be disappointed. Oh, that's just a pipedream. Get real!" So, as we mature physically, we become stunted spiritually. We learn to turn down or even shut off our creative drive. We learn we can't have what we want.

Learning how to create, how to re-awaken the imaginative urge we are born with, starts with understanding that we are worthy. Why *not* have what we want? We each have free will, we each have intelligence and existence and the ability to reason.

We have the means to be responsible for our choices. And we have a great power known as imagination. Every time we create, we become more aware of who we are and our capabilities. Every time we conceive an idea and bring it to fruition, we produce life. Unlike animals, as human beings who think and reason and imagine, when we create new life we also create awareness. We are life becoming aware of itself.

Benjamin Franklin is an excellent example of a man whose creative endeavors developed his Self awareness. Like Thomas Jefferson and Leonardo da Vinci, Franklin was truly a "Renaissance Man" of many talents — a writer, editor, scientist, inventor, statesman, ambassador, publisher, printer, and philosopher. He is a remarkable figure whose optimism, sense of humor and practical wisdom have been handed down through proverbs like "Diligence is the mother of good luck." Franklin dedicated his life to the continual improvement of himself. In his autobiography he describes a life plan he devised for attaining perfection. Each morning, Franklin would arise and ask himself the question, "What good will I do today?" He identified thirteen virtues which he believed to encompass the human perfection he desired: temperance, silence, order, resolution, frugality, industry, sincerity, justice, moderation, cleanliness, tranquility, chastity, and humility. Franklin chose one virtue a week to practice with diligence and recorded his progress daily. At the end of each day, he would review what he had learned, how he had evolved, and would ask himself the question, "What good did I do today?" and meditate upon this. Cultivating one virtue a week, practicing to develop it every day, Franklin repeated this cycle four times a year every year of his life. He was reportedly a very happy man, and attributed his happiness to this philosophy: "The most acceptable service to God is doing good to man."

Benjamin Franklin understood the principle that aiding others to abundance produces abundance in oneself. One of his most famous inventions, the Franklin stove, bears his name, but he never applied for a patent for it because he said, "As we enjoy great advantages from the inventions of others we should be glad of an opportunity to serve others by any invention of ours." He dedicated his life to public service from which he received no income after he retired at the age of forty-two from his publishing business, because he wanted to continue to give to others and to shape the course of human events with his ingenuity and practicality.

This example shows us that the secret to happiness does not lie in acquiring material things. We can use creative imagery for physical objects, to produce desired conditions, and to achieve status and recognition. The kind of creation that brings us the greatest joy, however, is that which brings us closer to our own creative essence. As we create, we discover more about our own wisdom, power, limitlessness, and originality. We learn what is infinite and eternal. We find out what links us with all of humanity, for we all emanate from the same origin. When we create for the purpose of understanding our own creative nature, we build security, for the laws of creation are just, immutable, and timeless. The thrill of connecting with that eternal source of creativity inspires us to strive to become the best we can be.
Every time we create responsibly, we are honoring the creative power, the essence of life itself. Think about what you love to do the most — do you sing to yourself when you are driving or walking? Do you draw in the margins of papers? Are you always writing letters or finding some other reason to write? When you are doing what you love, you are tapping into the creative genius within you. You are drawing from the inner source of your being. The process of creation itself will aid you to understand and know your worth. Every individual is unique, each one of us has special talents, abilities, understandings, qualities and skills to offer to the world. All of humanity is different today because we benefit from the creative gifts of musicians, scientists, educators, and leaders who followed their heart's desire. When you create what you love, you give the world a precious gift: *you!* You create your identity as you create the projects in your hands.

Take a moment to remember a time when you were happy, a time when you were in love with life, when you were attracted to another person, or a job, or a place you lived. What were you creating? Were you in the process of writing a novel? Painting a picture? Designing a home? Creating a successful business? There was some kind of imaginative thinking occurring that produced the thrill. The experience of being "in love" is one of being creative. Most people in love start to imagine marriage and often dream of having children together. Children are the offspring of a creative union. Whether our "children" are physical children or creative projects, the desire to produce offspring is the expression of our creative urge.

Every creation is a manifestation and expression of love. Love is a magnetic, attractive force. In its highest form, love brings life to our creations and springs forth from those creations. The seeds of all great works have their origin in love. Love is a drawing together of aggressive (masculine) and receptive (feminine) energies. When you give your attention to what you love it is easy to create. When you create it is easy to love what you do. The good feeling that comes from loving your life and creativity is not the temporary feeling that arises from emotional mood swings. The contentment and thrill of creating is a sustained, enduring, permanent satisfaction. Our creations come from within us and we have the power to create at will, any time we desire. There is a great security in knowing how the creative process works because we can apply what we have learned from one situation in life to another situation that is outwardly very different. For example, Martha was a very gifted pianist who was also extremely shy. She had practiced the piano from the time she was five, and over the years had developed a style uniquely hers. Martha was confident in that one area of her life, but was painfully insecure in meeting people and interacting with them. Martha's friend Elise asked her if she would be willing to teach piano lessons to her daughter. Martha hesitated at first but then agreed because Elise was her friend and she did not want to disappoint her. When Martha started teaching, she started to discover how she had developed her expertise with the piano, through a step by step process of discipline. Identifying these steps awakened within Martha a new awareness. She began to realize that just as she had learned to coordinate her hands, had learned to hear the music in her mind before she played the instrument, she could also learn to coordinate other aspects of herself. She realized that shyness was not a permanent state of being, and she could learn to become familiar with people and image different kinds of relationships than she had previously had. Playing the piano was not just a physical skill, it was an art that required the use of Martha's mind, imagination, and will, and these could be harnessed for her to shape a new quality of expression.

Knowing that you are a creative being gives you tremendous freedom. It means that you can move toward what you want rather than being paralyzed by fear or self doubt. It is a sad state in modern society that so many are separated from the creative urge within themselves. Too many people have learned that they are powerless and limited by conditions around them. Listen to people talk, and you will hear, "I can't help it, I'm only human. It's just not possible. I've got to struggle to survive. What's the point of trying to improve? Things will always go wrong in the end. I'm just one person. What can I do?" If you find yourself thinking this way, draw upon the examples of those whose single lifetime influenced the course of humanity — the Benjamin Franklins, Leonardo DaVincis, Marie Curies and Albert Einsteins. Imagine yourself being like they were and cause this to come about. As spiritual beings, we are endowed with creative imagination. We have free will, which means that we can always choose the conditions and circumstances in which we live. We are free to change the conditions that trouble us and with applied effort we can change negative ways of thinking that cloud the beauty of the soul.

To say or think "I can't" denies the very nature of our being. Thinking of life as a struggle for physical survival is saying existence is only for maintaining the physical body. But the life of the thinker is motion, creation, the use of imagination and free will. When we are using our imagination and free will we are alive! We are enthralled with life! A simple way to begin experiencing the joy of creation is to look every day for small ways that you can improve the world around you. When you walk down the street and see a piece of paper on the ground, pick it up. Smile at the people you see on the bus. Strike up a conversation with the woman behind you in the supermarket check-out line. Offer to lend a hand to a neighbor who is carrying a load into their home from their car. When you start looking for ways to help people and to cause positive changes, you will be amazed to discover how much you have to give. You will find that these small acts of kindness, practiced consistently throughout the day, will leave you with a sense of pride, well-being and self respect. In this way you will learn to believe in yourself. You will find out that you are worthy of receiving your desires.

To overcome a sense of purposelessness or meaning-lessness, to re-awaken the wonder and awe of life, decide how you want to be remembered. Do you want to be unreliable, full of good ideas that never amount to anything, or always falling short of your ideals? Of course not! You probably want to be remembered for being a person anyone could trust, an individual whose integrity and example helped to make the world a better place to be. Eleanor Roosevelt described it well: "If at the end one can say, 'This man used to the limit the powers that God granted him; he was worthy of love and respect and of the sacrifices of many people, made in order that he might achieve what he deemed to be his task,' then that life has been lived well and there are no regrets." Learn how to love what you do or create change in your life to do what you love. You have vast creative power within you, and the freedom to decide how you want to use it. Start now by asking yourself these questions: What do I want? What is life to me? How can I imagine being fulfilled? What is my greatest love? What is my greatest dream? What do I want to become? How do I want to influence the world? Give yourself time to explore these questions and reach deep within yourself for answers that resound with a sense of surety.

Give yourself the gift of discovery. Begin to experiment with a new way of thinking. Be purposeful. Think the kind of thoughts that will produce the peace and contentment you desire. We each have the ability to imagine, and through using imagi-nation we can create the life we desire for ourselves. Every time we create we learn that we are a part of something much greater than ourselves, for all the forces of the universe are on our side and draw to us seemingly mystical and magical experiences. We find out that everything we do affects someone else, and the more fully we give, the more expansive our influence becomes. This brings us happiness because improving the lives of others is one way of expressing gratitude for the gift of life. Every thought and action that is directed toward understanding *how creation occurs* will aid you to know your True Self. You will discover and expand your awareness of your True Self with each creative activity to which you give purposeful, attentive thought.

You will learn to transcend the insecurity of wondering "Why does this happen to me?" to knowing how you have created conditions and circumstances in your life. You will mature from a passive object, a victim of circumstance, to an active, creative subject who is fashioning his or her existence and identity. When you know how to create, you can reproduce your successes at will. You can expand your consciousness to embrace and understand Universal Truth. Instead of thinking that fortunate occurrences are "lucky" and out of your control, you will learn how to command the Universal Laws to cause mental, spiritual, and material evolution. When you make a mistake, instead of sinking into self pity, you will learn how to identify the cause and to make positive changes. You will know how to heal the conditions that plague you. You will develop greater self respect, confidence, and joy, truly becoming the director of your life.

*"How was Einstein able to conceive the Theory of Relativity?
He said the one crucial thing that helped him
was his ability to visualize:
"What would it be like
to be riding on the end of a light beam?"*
—*Anthony Robbins*

Universal Laws

Throughout this book there have been references made to the Universal Laws. Just as there are physical laws like gravity and relativity that govern the physical world, there are laws which govern the mental world we create in. In all existence there is structure, order, and form. This is true in the realm of creativity as well. The guidelines which define the order and structure of creation are called Universal Laws. They are universal because they apply to anyone, any time, any place. They do not discriminate. Because we all have minds and our minds are designed to work for us, each one of us has the ability to create our heart's desires by cooperating with the Universal Laws.

When you read books by or about successful people, you will find that there are similar ideas which permeate the literature. It doesn't matter what field of endeavor the notable person pursues—business, art, music, science, religion, communication — the same principles work. Even when someone does not know about the laws, even when they do not call them Universal Laws, they still use these universal principles. People who accomplish their ideals are cooperating with the Universal Laws whether they know it or not because the truth always prevails.

When you know about Universal Law, you will be more effective with your visualizing. You will be able to expend less energy and direct it more efficiently, enabling you to create always higher and greater achievements. You will invest your mental, emotional, and physical energy wisely because you will produce the results you desire. I will present some of the Universal Laws here for your use. Please understand that these are not all, and through the practice of daily mental and spiritual discipline you will develop greater awareness of the Universal Laws—what they are and how to use them. You will find these laws described in success literature, in the holy scripture of all religions, in mythology, in fairy tales, fables, and allegories that describe the essence and nature of man.

The Law of Believing and Knowing

This is a law practiced by many people in their everyday lives and stated in different words by philosophers of all kinds. Ralph Waldo Emerson said, "They conquer who believe they can." Nobel prize physicist Arthur H. Compton declared, "Every great discovery I ever made, I gambled that the truth was there, and then I acted on it in faith until I could prove its existence." Believing and knowing encapsulates the essence of creative imagery. A belief occurs when you have completely imaged something. You believe it is going to rain because the sky looks dark and cloudy and you can imagine the clouds turning to rain. You may hear a weather forecast that predicts rain when it is clear and sunny outside and think, "Oh, I don't believe that. It looks too nice to rain." It is hard for you to *imagine* impending rain when the sky is so blue.

In order to activate visualization in your life, start with learning how to *create* belief. When there is something you desire, listen to your thoughts. Do you expect to have your desire? Or do you have difficulty believing it is possible? Creating belief means creating a clear, complete thought-form image, incorporating all of your senses in the creation of the image. You can imagine just what your object of desire would look, smell, taste, feel, and sound like. When the thought form is complete, you have created a belief! I guarantee you, it will be easy for you to *believe* in the reality of your thought when it is formed in detail. The difficulty most people have in believing is that they have never created a complete image of the desired result. Because their desire is vague, it remains "wishful thinking" rather than a strong, firm belief. The Law of Believing and Knowing states that when you believe an idea you accept it into yourself. It is *real* and all it requires is your physical activity to cause it to become physical. The knowing comes about through the physical activity, for once your thought is physical you *know* or experience it. The key to using the Law of Believing and Knowing, therefore, is to create a complete, detailed thought-form image and act upon it until your desired thought is manifested into physical reality.

Watch children and listen to them. In their innocence, they readily believe that they can have what they imagine. There was a young girl named Kathy who wanted more than anything in the world to have a pony. She had friends who had horses and from the time she was six years old she frequented the stables, petting the horses, learning how to take care of them, to brush their coats, and when she got big enough she learned how to ride. She asked her parents for a pony, and her father told her that they had saved money for her college education in a trust fund that would be accessible when she turned eighteen. If she wanted to use that money for a horse she could. Kathy was disappointed because she didn't want to wait so many years. The more time she spent at the stables, the more she wanted a horse of her own. She loved the way they smelled, she loved to touch their warm coats, she thrilled at the power she felt when she rode. At seven years old, Kathy started finding ways to make money. She raised pet mice in her bedroom and sold them to the local pet store and to the neighborhood children. She did any odd jobs that she could and saved every penny she earned. Kathy also talked about her desire for a pony, and many of the adults she knew gave her gifts of money to put toward her pony. One summer, Kathy was given the use of a pony to keep and take care of and ride. It was used during the school year at a riding school and she was allowed to keep it when there were no classes in the summer. Caring for the pony, Kathy developed an even stronger image of having her own. She got up at the crack of dawn each day to feed it, brushed it regularly, cleaned out its stall, watered it, and loved it.

Finally, when Kathy was twelve years old, she had saved enough money to buy her own pony. When she rode it, she was ecstatic. It was exactly as she had imagined! Her story illustrates the importance of creating a strong image and holding on to it. It also shows that with will power and directed effort anything you imagine can come into being. Other children might have given up or they might have gotten distracted from their ideal, but Kathy continued to believe and invest her time and effort over a period of five years to fulfill her desire.

When you use Believing and Knowing the physical activity you put forth is worthwhile. If you find yourself at times becoming lazy or having difficulty motivating yourself to act on your desires, it is probably because you do not believe your actions will pay off. You think, "Why bother?" because you haven't imagined yourself receiving your desires, or you even imagine yourself being rejected or disappointed. When you initiate your creations with a clearly defined thought-form image, your time and activity is an investment which you know will pay off because it is directed toward the completion of your visualized object of desire. With practice you will discover that your thoughts are things and you will discover the reality of mind substance. Belief creates more belief, for the more you practice imagining first and following it with activity, the more you will know how to reproduce success in your life.

If you have difficulty believing in yourself, if you think that there are some people who live a "charmed life" and that you are one of the "unlucky" people who never achieve their desires, consider this. The Universal Laws are universal, therefore, if they can work for the "charmed" person they can work for you, too. You don't even need to believe in yourself as long as you believe in the efficacy of the Laws. They are unchangeable, and will work whether you are up or down, excited or depressed, feeling good about yourself or not. They are not affected by your changeable emotional states. They function equally for people of all ages, races, cultures, and religions. What security! You can rely on the Universal Laws through all the changes of your temporary physical existence. You do need to be willing to imagine what you want and to act in accordance with your visualized image. The Laws are no substitute for effort! The great thinker Thomas Alva Edison knew that "Genius is 1% inspiration and 99% perspiration." Remember that when you are tempted to give up with the excuse that you are not good enough or smart enough or resourceful enough to fulfill your fondest dreams. With practice, you will discover that you can command the laws and you will build a greater sense of self respect and self worth.

Here is an example of how the Law of Believing and Knowing worked for me. Years ago, after having completed a first course of study in metaphysics, I wanted to teach others what I had learned. I did not have great belief in myself, but I believed strongly in the value of the teachings I received, and I had used the mental exercises and principles in the lessons to make some dramatic changes in my life. It was very important to me to share these teachings, to give to people what I had been given by my teachers.

I created a very strong thought-form image of what I had found to be valuable—the practice of concentration, the stillness and quiet of meditation, the profound awareness I had gained from learning to interpret dreams, the calmness I had developed from learning how to recharge and re-energize my body, the security that had come from the daily practice of mental discipline, the joy of creating my physical and spiritual desires. I visualized myself giving to everyone in the community, for I wanted everyone to know what I knew. I went over to the School of Metaphysics every day, sat in the teacher's chair, and visualized every seat in the classroom being filled with a student who was eager to learn. I made posters about the class starting, and as I wrote the phone number of the school on each one, I projected the image of the value of the class, so that I was permeating the paper with my strong thought-form desire to share what I had learned.

I believed that this was the best education anyone could receive. I wrote letters to people who had previously contacted the school for lectures and other services, introducing myself and the class. After I addressed the letters, I held each one in my hand. I visualized a light beginning in the center of my being, at my solar plexus region, imaged expanding it until I was flooded with brilliant light, then I radiated the letter with my light as I thought, "Welcome to the light" to the person receiving the letter. Then I imagined embracing the recipient with light, enfolding them in it while they absorbed its warmth. I imaged the person responding, "Yes! This is what I have been looking for." The first night of the class, I was sitting in the teacher's chair while the students were filling out a registration questionnaire. As I looked around the room, I realized that this image was exactly what I had visualized—every seat in the classroom was filled with a student who was curious and eager to learn! My belief had become a knowing.

Law of Abundance

He who aids others to abundance will always have abundance. This is an infallible law. You may have heard the folk wisdom, "If you feed a man a fish you've fed him for a day. Teach him *how* to fish and you've fed him for a lifetime." This is another expression of this law.

Using the Law of Abundance will bring great joy into your life. It will ease your frustrations and give you the means to create the kind of world in which you want to live. What is abundance? An overflowing, never ending supply of all that you need. When you use your resources to the fullest, you will have a rich harvest in your own life. When you aid others to do the same, they will also experience their life flourishing. When everyone reaches out to help his or her neighbor, the whole world prospers. Imagine a world with infinite, limitless resources. Imagine your own Self as a vast source of eternal truth. With unbounded resources within and without, it becomes easy to image that you can always find what you need to create what you want!

The Law of Abundance provides the means for you to receive into your life more than you have at the present. When you visualize, you are putting together in a new way energy and substance that is already present in your mind and your life. As you create, as you form images, you transform the energy and substance into a new form. Abundance means that you always have more than enough to fulfill your needs. As you use resources to their fullest, you will make use of all the energy and substance that is available to you. As you aid others to abundance, you will insure that the energy you use is recycled so that there is a continual supply.

How do you use resources to the fullest? There are many simple examples. Change the washers in the sink so that you use the water you need and do not have a drippy faucet that wastes water. Plan your shopping trips so that in one trip you buy groceries, get gas, and pick up the kids from school rather than running back and forth. You will save time and energy (your own and the car's.) Use scrap paper to write notes to yourself and use the good office stationary for business correspondence. Recycle glass and cans. Look for the ways that you can practice conserving energy. When you eliminate waste, you will be amazed to find out how bountiful the universe is! You will not worry about running out of time, energy, or money. Because you are fully using the energy available to you, you will easily imagine that there are copious resources to fulfill your desires. Determine the difference between your wants and your needs. There is so much material substance available in the physical world, it is easy to become distracted by endless desires. Clothes, toys, cars, boats, televisions...the list of physical possessions could go on and on. Ask yourself, is this something I *need* to be happy? Or is this something I *want?* The more you learn how to cultivate Self awareness, the more you will evolve and learn what provides eternal bliss and what supplies a temporary reward. Why waste your time and energy pursuing desires that will soon become meaningless? It is wiser to invest in permanent treasures.

The understandings you gain become a permanent part of you. Offer the wisdom you have gained from your own life experiences to others. By aiding other people to abundance, you ensure that your influence extends beyond you. When you know how something works, teach this. Many parents want their children to have it easier than they had it themselves, so they do not always teach them how to clean or cook or take care of the mundane tasks of life. When the children move out on their own, they have a difficult time because they do not know how to take care of themselves. Although it may take a little bit more time in the beginning to teach a child how to perform theses tasks, in the long run it will save time for the parent (who will then have greater freedom to attend to other tasks themselves). It will also benefit the child who can then live more effectively and be a contributing member of society.

This is a simple illustration of the importance of sharing, one of the keys to abundance. Most of us have been taught to share our physical possessions. Children learn this from sharing their toys with friends or siblings. But how many of us are taught to share our knowledge and wisdom? <u>The greatest gift you can offer to the world is *you*.</u> When you pass on to other people what you have learned, you benefit the lives of many. Each person you touch in turn touches many other people. When all people share their inner wealth with one another we have a much more prosperous world. Using the Law of Abundance will help you to create your desires for you will find that you learn more about what you know when you teach it to someone else. You will hear yourself say something, and as you hear it a light will come on in your mind. "Aha! So that's how it works!" These "Aha!" experiences create greater abundance in your own life, for you will discover truths that you did not even know you knew, and then you will be able to apply these truths to other areas of your life. Judy discovered this when she taught a writing class. Judy had been a writer for some thirty years, but had never had the opportunity to teach this. Her own practice of writing had evolved over the years, from learning vocabulary and basic grammar, to reading many different authors, to writing essays, learning to write poetry, and eventually writing short stories. When Judy had the opportunity to teach a class in creative expression, she drew upon memory to separate the steps she had taken, and was overwhelmed to discover that she had put together much understanding herself that had never been directly taught to her by a teacher. Judy found out through teaching her writing class that writing was not simply knowing words and knowing how to put them together. Good writing came from being attentive to life, using the senses to receive, observing people and determining their character from their actions, and then recording these perceptions with words. Judy had not even realized how perceptive and observant she was until she began teaching these skills. This was enlightening, as it helped her find out some of her strengths that she had taken for granted.

The Law of Abundance will give you the means to form the kind of world you want to live in. Have you ever wished other people were more kind, or more disciplined, or more truthful? Perhaps these are qualities you have and could show others how to develop. Maybe you know something they do not, and you can be of service through your example, teaching, or words of truth. When I was growing up, I was taught consideration by my parents. I learned to respect other people's time, their things, and their personal space. As I grew older, I found myself often in situations with other people who had not learned that same kind of respect. They would be very demanding, and I would become angry with them for being so inconsiderate. For many years I "stewed" when another person was inconsiderate. Finally, it dawned on me that some of these people didn't even know they were being inconsiderate. Some of them were oblivious to anything other than their own needs and desires. When I communicated my desires, it surprised them. They hadn't thought about someone else having needs, too. They had never learned to consider another person in their thoughts and actions. Although it wasn't easy at first for me to communicate in this way, it was productive. It put me in a position to aid someone else to expand their thinking, to include other people within the scope of their awareness. And it aided me to become more aware of what I was taking for granted in myself. Through giving I received enhanced understanding. Thus, as I aided another to abundance I received abundance myself.

All of the great masters, religious and political leaders were people who understood this concept. They were public servants who devoted time and energy to aiding their fellow man. Through service to humanity, dedicated people like these become enlightened. They learn that we are all part of the same creation, and as one individual grows and develops he or she enhances the whole. Each one of us can contribute to help others and in so doing all of us live a more exalted life.

Law of Proper Perspective

Too many things to do and not enough time to do them? Learn how to put first things first! The Law of Proper Perspective means determining what is most important to you and what will produce soul growth. Activating the Law of Proper Perspective starts with some deep thinking. What is life to you? Why do you approach it? What produces the greatest satisfaction and security for yourself? If you were to die tomorrow, what would you want to have accomplished and produced with your life? With these questions in mind, you can begin to decide what to do first. What desires will you need to accomplish first, second, third, and so on. This is a very important law because you can fulfill many desires in your life only when you put them in order. Without order, you become scattered and run around like a chicken with your head cut off!

Jane is a good example of a woman who had many desires and needed to use proper perspective to accomplish them all. She wanted a good education, she wanted to be married and to have children, and she wanted a successful career. To prioritize her goals, Jane examined the purpose for each one. Her purpose for receiving an education was to find out about the world, to learn more about other people's ways of thinking, and to become acquainted with areas of life she had not previously encountered. Jane decided that pursuing her education first would be proper perspective, as it would give her knowledge that would aid her in deciding what kind of career would be most fulfilling. Jane did know that she wanted to be married before having children, out of respect for them, to raise them in an established family environment. But she was not sure if she wanted to be married before establishing her career or get her career going first. Jane determined that the purpose for a career was a means to express herself, a place to be creative, to establish her identity, and to learn about her own talents and skills. She decided, therefore, to pursue the career before marriage because she wisely assessed the importance of establishing security in herself individually before building a relationship with another. She wanted to bring a sense of individual wholeness into her marriage rather than attempting to seek fulfillment through a mate who would define her identity. Jane also believed that her education and career would help her to build the kind of maturity that would enable her to be a good wife and mother, thus those two goals needed to come before marriage and motherhood. Jane's purpose for marriage was to develop good communication skills, to understand how to become close with another individual, to learn to be committed, and to share herself intimately with another. She knew that developing these interpersonal skills would aid her in being a good parent. She wanted to establish a good relationship with her husband before planning to have children so that she and her husband would be united in their ideals once the children were born. Jane's understanding of proper perspective aided her in determining the importance of establishing her own goals before bringing children into the world. She wanted to know how to fulfill her own desires and how to be creative and successful first, so that she could guide her children from experience and teach them with integrity. She wanted to learn to be disciplined herself before teaching them discipline, and wanted to let her children be individuals rather than trying to live vicariously through them. She created a life plan — education first, career second, marriage third, children fourth— by visualizing the kind of conditions and understandings she wanted to have.

With proper perspective you can learn planning. You can learn to use your time, money, and energy most efficiently. A good way to practice proper perspective is with cooking. In this modern day of instant coffee and microwave ovens, it is easy to forget that there are steps in any creation. Who knows what to do first when they have learned to pop a box in the microwave oven and that's dinner? When you practice cooking, you learn to start first with the foods that take the longest to cook. Second, you cook what will be the next longest. And so on. With the use of visualization, you can determine in what order to cook the foods so that they are all finished at the same time. The result is a carefully orchestrated meal. This is a simple, physical way to visualize a whole event (the meal) comprised of parts or steps. You can apply this to any endeavor that at first seems over-whelming. Visualize the whole picture and then break it down into parts. This can be a life plan, like Jane's, or a weekend plan that includes shopping, recreation, homework, and time spent with family. It can be planning for a big event like a wedding or a business seminar — any endeavor in life! You can begin to practice this each day by making a "To Do" list. Write down daily everything that you want and need to accomplish. At first, you may want to write down the activities in the order they "come to mind." Then, go over your list and number in order of priority what is most important to do first, second, third, and so on. Perform each of these activities in this order, and as you accomplish them, cross them off the list. This will help you to build pride and confidence, as you watch yourself being competent and responsible. It will also help you to note when you are procrastinating. You may find that there is an activity you keep skipping over and adding to your next day's "To Do" list. This is a clue to you that you are putting off the activity! See if you can break it down into smaller parts so that you can take a first step in its accomplishment.

You will learn proper perspective by discovering how each individual goal or activity fits into the larger scheme of things. That is why it is important to consider what your life means to you. When it is all said and done, when you are about to rest for the evening or for the end of your life, what do you want to have completed? How do the daily activities that face you relate to this grander ideal in life? When you see how one step leads to another you begin to understand the importance of each individual step.

Law of Cause and Effect

In the metaphysical realm, thought is cause and effect is its manifest likeness. In other words, you are as you image yourself to be. You create your reality with thought. As we have shown, your subconscious mind can only reproduce what your conscious mind creates. Therefore, what you experience in your life is the effect (results) of your thinking.

Putting this law into practice will give you a way to understand true responsibility. The first responsibility you have is to your Self—to respond to the desires of your soul. Your soul craves maturity. Your conscious mind and physical self crave comfort. When you make choices that will produce maturity for your soul, you will be learning and growing and therefore content. When you make choices to feed your physical self only, you set yourself up for disappointment. For example, there were two men we will call Joe and Bob. Both Joe and Bob had worked for many years in the same company and both were offered the opportunity to transfer to a new city to open a branch of the company. Joe and Bob were excited at first. The prospect of meeting new people and facing new challenges was exciting. Both had become somewhat bored in their old jobs and had even thought about the need for a new stimulus to bring back the zest in life. Joe responded well to the challenge. In his new position, he got to develop leadership skills he had not used before. He learned how to investigate the community and to scope out resources for new client contacts. He visited many local groups, schools, churches, and community events and made new friends. He found out that he was a likable person and how he could use his sincerity to draw similar people to him. Bob, on the other hand, created a different attitude. Although he was excited at first by the prospect of change, he did not image how he wanted to be different. He felt like he had been abandoned all alone in a new city where he knew no one. He felt sorry for himself and waited for people to introduce themselves to him. When that did not happen, he decided that he had moved to an unfriendly town and resented his boss for placing him there. The two men faced very similar circumstances but the difference was in their attitude. Joe wanted to learn, to reach out and to meet new people. He wanted to learn about himself and what he could share in a new way and in a new place. Bob knew that he wanted a change, as he had been bored in his old job, but he never imagined how *he* would change. So even though he experienced a change in circumstances, he brought with him the kind of isolation that had contributed to his dissatisfaction in the previous location.

You may have heard about "karma." Karma is a Sanskrit word which means "indebtedness as an individual." The debt you owe is to yourself—to fill your soul with understandings of creation. When you continually repeat experiences and ask "Why does this keep happening to me?" it is because your soul or Self desires to learn. You keep creating a particular kind of situation and circumstance to provide conditions for learning. It is your duty to create learning to relieve the karma. Karma is caused by your intention and relieved by your understandings. In Bob's case, it was his karma to be in the new location where he knew no one, not because he was being punished by some cosmic force, but because his soul wanted to learn to give, to influence, and to share. Bob continually found himself in situations where he was alone. He was left by his wife, he had been transferred to different locations when he was in the army, and each time he thought that he had been abandoned. He missed close relationships, not because everyone left him, but because he needed to reach out to others. With a more positive attitude, Bob could begin to see these similar circumstances as an opportunity to give, to be himself, to create his identity as a loving and influential person.

To cause learning means creating an idea of what you want to change. For example, I found myself continually involved with individuals who had little money. I felt sorry for them, and loaned them money so that they could get back on their feet. However, after awhile I started to resent this, and also found that I did not receive back most of the money I was "lending." At first I got engrossed in self pity. "Why does this happen to me?" I asked, and I blamed the people to whom I was lending the money. Then I started to become honest when I realized that *I* was the one who kept lending the money. They didn't force me! Why? What were my intentions? I realized that in most cases the loans were my way of keeping strings attached to the people to whom I was giving the money. As long as I kept lending them money they were dependent on me. Furthermore, the pity I practiced (feeling sorry for them) was blatant lack of respect for them and for myself. If I could work to make enough money to lend it to them, they could work too. They were as strong and capable as I.

When I became honest with these intentions, I was faced with a choice. I could continue to practice disrespect ("Oh, you poor thing. You can't help it if you have overspent your money.") I could continue to practice disrespecting myself by being "victimized" by people who never paid back the loans. Or

I could change. When I imagined myself being asked for loans, I imaged a different response from the one I had previously used. I visualized myself saying no, and completed the conversation in my mind. Thus, when the situation arose, I followed through by practicing what I had imagined. This caused a change in my behavior and set the stage for causing a change in my understanding of self respect and respect for others.

In using the Law of Cause and Effect, the more purposeful you are, the more control you will have. In the example related, I caused a change only after experiencing effects I considered unpleasant. It is more direct and more productive to cause change with foresight. Visualize what understandings you want to build and create the conditions and circumstances which will afford you the opportunities to do so. A positive way to direct the Law of Cause and Effect is to think, "I create my world around me." Be the kind of person you want to be (for example, good, kind, loving) and you will create an atmosphere conducive to its expression. You will learn to see that in every situation there is a gift for you — an opportunity to learn, to become more complete, to develop understanding, patience, compassion, self respect, and so forth. Every experience in your life will take on greater meaning and purpose.

Law of Attraction

A couple of years ago I was attending an exercise class at a health club near my home. I really enjoyed the instructor because her love for teaching and concern for her students was evident. After the class ended, I went up to her to thank her for teaching and to find out when she taught other classes so I could attend. I told her I traveled quite a bit with my job so I was not always in town to come to her classes. She asked me what I do, and I told her that I am a teacher at the School of Metaphysics and continued to describe what metaphysics teaches. Her eyes grew wide and she said, "Wow! That's amazing. I love that stuff. In fact, a couple of the other girls who work here keep a book behind the counter that lists dream symbols and when we have free time we talk about each others' dreams. One of the other women who had attended the class overheard us speak, and when she heard "dreams" she said, "You know, I heard someone on the radio yesterday morning interpreting dreams and what she said made more sense than anything I had ever heard before about dreams." I asked her what station she was listening to, and then smiled and said, "That was me you heard on the radio." She said, "Really?" and several of us discussed dreams and their interpretations for about an hour. Susan, the instructor, came over to the School of Metaphysics that evening to register for a new class starting. Was this some divine accident that caused all of us to be in the same place at the same time? Or was it a response to some mysterious plan?

What causes a coincidence to occur? How do seemingly miraculous events take place? The action of attraction is one of the forces at work! When you create a clear, complete, and detailed thought form, you have created a seed idea. With attention and concentration, you can cause a thought form to be planted in the fertile soil of your subconscious mind. In order for your seed idea to grow, you must release your attention from it. Once your thought has become embedded in the soil of your subconscious mind, it begins to grow. You water it with physical activity directed toward the end result you desire, and give it sunlight by bathing it periodically with your attention and love. As your thought form grows, it attracts to it other energies and minds similarly conditioned. Have you ever heard the saying, "Like attracts like"? This is an expression of the Law of Attraction. When your thought form has been planted, it reaches out with thought waves to the entire universe. There is a universal mind in which all of our minds connect. There will always be other minds with desires and needs compatible to your own. These other minds are also creating visualized thought forms which reach out into universal mind. When these similar thought forms meet, the attraction produces a match. At the health club, my desire was to share with others what I have found to be true. The other two women who were interested in dreams had a desire to find a way to learn more about what their dreams mean. These compatible desires came together and we found each other by communicating our interests.

Like seeds growing in rich, fertile soil, a thought form

that is developing in the subconscious mind is imperceptible to the physical senses. When a seed is within the earth, you tend it and care for it although you cannot yet see, touch, feel, or smell it. In the same way, there is a time to watch expectantly for a developing thought form to manifest in physical form. Knowing that you have created a clear and complete image, you watch for the signs that your desired object is coming to fruition. The Law of Attraction operates even when you do not know exactly how you will fulfill a desire. It ensures that you will be in the right place at the right time for things to "click" into place.

I heard a minister named John relate a story describing his faith in divine providence, a true tale which illustrates the action of universal law. John had recently moved from a city to a rural area with his family. A hardworking man, he had not yet obtained a full time job to support his family although he willingly accepted any work which was available. One evening as dinnertime approached, John knew that there was no food to feed his family, but he instructed his daughter to set the table nonetheless. John believed that his efforts would pay off in some way at some time, he knew that he was a good person, and he knew that his family was worthy of being fed. He had had seemingly miraculous events occur at other times in his life and he trusted that the universe would not let his family go hungry. The family gathered together around the table and John led them in prayer. As they sat holding hands, there was a knock at the door. John finished the prayer and answered the door. There stood his landlord with two grocery sacks in his arms. The landlord was a gruff man who usually said very little and rarely smiled. John greeted him, and the landlord said, "Our garden is producing so many vegetables my wife and I can't keep up. I hate waste, so I was wondering if you would use any of these things. Oh, and we just butchered a steer and there are certain cuts my kids won't eat, so if you think yours would eat them, you can have these, too." John smiled gratefully and thanked his landlord, assuring him that the food would be put to good use. This story demonstrates the action of several universal laws, including the "match" of compatible desires — John's desire to feed his family and the landlord's desire to insure that the food to good use.

When events "just happen" to occur fortuitously, the Law of Attraction is at work. Here is an example. When I was directing a School of Metaphysics in Ann Arbor, Michigan I set a goal to start a new class in applied metaphysics at that center. I created a very clear image of the benefits of the lessons — learning concentration to become calm and centered, dream interpretation for self awareness, mental relaxation, greater direction in life, peace of mind. I created a strong idea of love, for I loved what I was learning and wanted to share it with others. I made telephone calls to people who had come to lectures at the school, put announcements in the newspaper, announced it to all my students who put out the word to their friends, posted notices around the local university campus. One day, as I returned from work, the phone rang. It was a woman who was asking all kinds of questions about the school and its services. I answered her questions, and then asked her how she had heard about the school. "That's the funniest thing," she replied. "I had just been thinking about how it was time to make a change in my life and I didn't know exactly what to do. One thing I've always found is that when I need to clear my mind I'll clean the house. It gives me a way to get my mind off my problems. Well, I was dusting the bookshelf, and I knocked the phone book off. It fell open to the yellow pages, and I saw your ad there. What a coincidence!"

This shows the Law of Attraction at work. I had formed a clear image of my desire to teach and this woman had formed a clear image of her desire to learn. Both of our minds were reaching out, and the desires "met" in Universal Mind. I want to point out that in both cases there was a physical response to the desire; in my case I was putting forth activity so that people would know the class was starting. In fact, someone before me had responded to a desire to teach and serve by placing the ad in the yellow pages. The woman responded to her desire by picking up the telephone and calling once she saw the ad. At any stage this "match" could have been thwarted if one or both people had been passive, or said defeatedly, "Why bother. It's not going to work anyway. "

Using the laws means that you create the desire in your

mind and respond with your physical activity. The Law of Attraction is fun to use, because in order to effect it you must watch expectantly. The thrill of discovery is apparent in every book you read, every corner you turn, every letter you open. Every time the phone rings, you may think, "Is this the one who is calling to come to class?" Every time you open the newspaper you can look for *your* job that will be advertised that day. Or whatever it is you desire — instead of wondering *if* it will happen, you look for *when* and *where* the signs of its manifestation are occurring. This makes living a joy, and exploring avenues of experience stimulating and rewarding.

The Law of Ten Fold Return

To have prosperity in your life you must expect it. Unfortunately, many people have been taught "it is better to give than receive" or "don't expect too much and you won't be disappointed." But when you think about this, does it make sense? If you give and give and never receive, you will soon be burnt out and resent giving. When you give, you benefit someone else and you receive rewards from the act of giving, for you give yourself a way to heighten your awareness of who you are and what you have to give. You may have learned to use the Law of Ten Fold Return in aphorisms like, "One good turn deserves another." When you do a good deed, you are giving, and you receive an immediate return in a heightened sense of pride, honor, and self respect. You do not expect your return from the person to whom you have given; you anticipate that you will receive a return somehow, from some source. It is easy to expect to receive from the abundance of the universe when you know that you have been generous.

Even when you give of your physical riches, you can expect to receive. The Law of Ten Fold Return states that when you give freely, you can expect to receive ten times what you have given, thus enabling you to give ten times more. Practicing the Law of Ten Fold Return will help you to create an attitude and experience of wealth. Start by giving an amount that you can easily release. Practice giving the same amount every day. Let's say you start by giving ten cents a day. Give this ten cents freely, anonymously if possible. When you give the ten cents, say out loud, "I hereby give this ten cents and claim my ten fold return for the goodness of all concerned!" Then, visualize yourself receiving a dollar bill. Practice this complete action, giving the money, releasing it, stating out loud the amount of your gift and claiming the ten fold return, and visualizing the return. You will then watch for how the money returns to you. As you practice receiving your return, you will find yourself having greater abundance and wealth and desiring to give larger amounts. Keep increasing the amounts you give as you increase the amounts you receive. It is said that the entrepreneur and millionaire John D. Rockefeller gave a shiny new dime to each new person he met, long before he had amassed his fortune. His life demonstrates his practice of the Law of Ten Fold Return. Even today the Rockefeller Foundation contributes large amounts of money to worthy causes.

Your ten fold return will come to you according to the value you place upon your gift and your expectation. If you think, "Oh, this is only a dime," and devalue its worth, you will have difficulty receiving a return. If you think, "This will never work," it won't. Even small amounts of money add up. Every penny you give will return to you tenfold. As you give, you will receive, and the more you give, the more you receive. The more you receive, the more you have to give. When you receive, give thanks for what you have received by giving. You will cause an infinite cycle of prosperity!

I have known many people who use the Law of Ten Fold Return. The first time I used it purposely, I was skeptical but was willing to try it out. I gave fifty cents to a charitable organization, and as I gave the money anonymously (so that there would be no strings attached), I said to myself, "I expect to receive five dollars." Then I forgot about it. Fifty cents was a small amount, so I was not worried about whether or not it would return, and my attitude was one of experimentation. A few days later, I went to a dance concert that I had wanted to attend for quite awhile. I hadn't bought a ticket in advance, and to my dismay, when I arrived the concert was sold out. I was standing in line with my friend, and we were discussing the situation. He decided to leave, since he was not particularly attached to seeing the concert. I decided to stay, thinking that maybe at the last minute there would be an extra ticket. The woman who was in front of us in the line overheard our conversation. After my friend left, she turned to me and said, "Do you need a ticket?" I said, "Yes, I do!" She said, "My husband was supposed to come with me but at the last minute he couldn't make it — here, you can have his ticket." I thanked her, and pulled out my wallet to pay her. She waved her hand and said, "Oh, no. It's yours. Just pass it on some time." I thanked her again for her generosity and thought no more about it until later that evening as I was walking home from the concert. The ticket had cost five dollars — exactly ten times the fifty cents I donated earlier in the week! When you use the Law of Ten Fold Return, give freely and watch for the return. Do not put conditions on how the return will come to you or you may limit how you receive.

Another example of tenfold return occurred with a group of people who were volunteering their time for a nonprofit organization. They had decided that they wanted to receive a large monetary donation to benefit the organization, but had not specified an amount. After considering the importance of creating clearly defined thought-form images, the director of the organization decided to start with a goal of $1000. She wrote this down and posted it for all of the members of the organization to see, so that all could participate in the visualization. Among the activities of this group was a fundraiser which the members created to generate money for operating expenses. They decided to hold a yard sale, but they needed items to sell. Several of the students read newspaper ads for other yard sales, and visited these sales requesting the leftover items for their own sale. The members of the group volunteered their time to pick up the items, and in a few weeks had collected enough items to hold a huge sale for their own group. The director of the organization instructed the members to tenfold the energy and time they volunteered.

When the sale was over, after having raised about $200, the participants wondered what to do with the leftover items. They called around to various groups and organizations to find out who could pick up the clothes, furniture, knicknacks, and other objects that remained. As they were calling, "coincidentally" a couple of young men came by who were members of a church that had a home for disadvantaged youths. These two young men asked if any of the items were available to be donated to their group. The director of the organization which had held the sale offered them all the items left over. The young men did not need all of it, but they offered their time and service to pick up everything left over, to keep what their group could use, and to bring what was left to the Salvation Army or Goodwill.

This was the first example of tenfold return. The time and energy the members of the group expended returned tenfold in the time and energy offered by the two men who belonged to the church. But this was not all! Two weeks after this event, a woman came over to the place which held the yard sale. She had been affiliated with this group at one time and had received many benefits from it. She spoke to the director for a few minutes, telling her how much she had received and how grateful she was. She said that she was going to leave a donation to show her appreciation. She dropped some bills in a jar that was labeled "donation." Later, when the director was about to make a bank deposit she reached into the jar and discovered that the "small" donation was thirteen one hundred dollar bills! This was even greater than the $1000 she had previously visualized and expected.

This story shows how visualization produces great success when coupled with the use of the Law of Ten Fold Return. When you give, you can always expect to receive, although you do not necessarily receive from the person or place to which you have given. When you think about giving, give freely, generously, and with love. Give as you would like others to give to you. This is the Golden Rule: "Do unto others as you would have them do unto you." You will receive multiplied in the manner with which you give.

Knowing that there are Universal Laws will help you in your use of visualization. When you practice creative imagery, you can draw upon power greater than your own. Forces unseen to your eyes and heard not by your ears are at work, ready to aid you to fulfill your desires. In the beginning, trust that these mysterious energies are available to you and as you experiment you will become more familiar with their beneficence. The German philosopher Goethe described this process with great eloquence:

"Until one is committed, there is hesitancy, the chance to draw back, always ineffectiveness. Concerning all acts of initiative (and creation), there is one elementary truth the ignorance of which kills countless ideas and splendid plans: *that moment one definitely commits oneself then Providence moves, too.*

"All sorts of things occur to help one that would never otherwise have occurred. A whole stream of events issues from the decision, raising in one's favor all manner of unforseen incidents and meetings and material assistance, which no man could have dreamed would have come his way.

"Whatever you can do or dream you can, begin it. Boldness has genius, power, and magic in it. Begin it now."

"A man's reach must exceed his grasp,
or what's a heaven for?"
— Robert Browning

Affirmations III

All people have aspirations. We all strive to become greater and better, and within each soul resides an element of hope. Some of us have been fortunate to have the kind of upbringing that cultivated our dreams, parents or teachers or coaches who encouraged us to develop our greatest potential. Some people have had ideals shattered, and have been thus stimulated to try harder, to be more determined to conquer any obstacle. Other people have accepted defeat, perceiving what could have been temporary setbacks as "signs" that their desires are not meant to be. All of us have the freedom to choose how we want to approach our lives. We can nurture the seeds of hope to create wonderful experiences, or we can bury them and settle for mediocrity or even despair.

We can bring a spark of life into our hearts and minds any time we need or want to. Even when we are depressed, when things are not going as we would like, when it seems that everything we try does not work, we still have an effective, powerful and reliable resource: creative imagery. We can imagine ourselves into a new way of thinking and a new state of being. Everyone has experienced moments of inspiration that brought home the splendor of our universe. I can remember driving through a horrendous rainstorm, the sky black with thunderclouds and with such a torrential downpour it was impossible to see the road. The prospect of driving for several more hours through the storm filled me with dread. I prayed, "Please let the rain stop so that I have a clear and safe drive." Soon, the darkness in the sky lifted a little and the heavy rain became a sprinkle. Amidst the grey clouds a band of color appeared. The faint beginning of a rainbow! I was cheered. As I gazed at it, I marveled that there would be a rainbow so late in the day, as it was about 8:00 p.m. I supposed that this was how sunset appeared through clouds. The rainbow gave me hope that the rest of my drive would be pleasant. I continued to watch it as I drove, and wondered why none of the other drivers seemed to notice. Then, as I gazed out the windshield I noticed that the band of color was extending. What had been a faint ribbon peeking through the thick grey clouds was now a complete arch, 180° spanning the sky. It was like a miracle, to see this magnificent display of nature's beauty. It reminded me that there is something wonderful in every experience, and even when things seem bleak there is the potential for beauty, splendor, and grace.

You have probably had your own moments of awe-inspiring wonder. Perhaps it was listening to a Mozart sonata or a stirring rendition of Handel's Messiah. Maybe it was the birth of a child, or a solemn vow of commitment at a wedding. You may have contemplated nature's supreme harmony in the stillness of dawn. Experiences like these stimulate a sense of connectedness, knowing that we are a part of something greater than ourselves. When we are "at one" with the presence of a power or energy of such magnitude, we are enriched and nourished. We experience great peace and joy.

Rather than waiting for these "peak experiences" to happen to us, we can learn to cause them. We can create a centered, calm awareness through creative imagery and make it a part of our consciousness with daily affirmation. Many spiritual disciplines invoke the power of sound to create a state of higher consciousness. Some chant hymns or repeat mantras. Most parents are aware of the soothing nature of the voice, as they sing or croon to their infants to lull them to sleep. Anyone who has heard the majestic blending of tones in a symphony or choral presentation knows how music can stir passion. You, too, can use the sense of sound to produce vibrations conducive to a particular way of thinking.

In using affirmations to awaken higher ideals, begin with causing stillness in your mind. Practice holding your attention in one place by choosing a single word to repeat to yourself. A word like "love" or "peace" or "power" or "still" or "joy" will be effective. Choose a word which describes a state of mind you want to cultivate. Say the word out loud, listen to the sounds roll off your tongue and resonate in your diaphragm, throat, and head. Image the thought of *love* as you say the word. Use an image that is real to you. Use the same word rather than switching from one to another. The repeated, daily practice of sounding the word and imaging it is like digging a hole in the ground. As you dig deeper and deeper you will come closer to your Real Self. You do not want to have many shallow ditches by saying different words for brief periods of time. You can chant the word when you are alone, or you can repeat it silently to yourself when you are in the presence of others. Any time you want to call upon the state of higher awareness, sound your thought form.

You will find that repeating the word-sound will bring you comfort. The thought of *love,* for example, will grow stronger and clearer as you say it and you will become more loving as you image and practice love. You will at first become acquainted with the many facets of the quality you are cultivating, and it will soon become your friend. Then you can move on to develop other attitudes and qualities. Choose a word for your core thought which you will begin to use daily. Use a word that resonates within you, which stimulates an idea that is appealing to you. Joy, love, light, integrity, divinity — whatever word you choose, create a clear and strong image as you repeat the vibration and it will become a part of your being with practice.

Following are the affirmations which have already been introduced in this book. Within these affirmations are many words you might use for your core vibration. This time, read each affirmation out loud. Hear the sounds as you say the words and as you image the thought. Know that you are invoking the power of Universal Law as you create the thought of yourself being connected with all of humanity. Each one of these affirmations will help you to discover your place in the universe, for they stimulate you to recognize your duty to make the world a better place. As you do so, you become personally enriched. You will find out that the greatest wealth you possess is within yourself, and as you share with others you understand the great depth and providence of creation!

> *I am happy, creative, and fulfilled.*
> *Life is full of unlimited resources.*
> *Wherever I am, good things happen.*
> *I am full of joy.*
> *I give thanks for the treasures in my life.*
> *It is a wonderful day!*
> *I love my life.*
> *I give thanks for abundance and prosperity.*
> *I look for the gift in every experience.*
> *I am ready and willing to receive life's abundance.*
> *I love the divinity in each person I meet.*
> *I salute the divinity within you.*
> *I improve the earth plane wherever I go.*
> *I am a fountain of joy.*
> *I give ever-increasing riches from the source*
>   *of my abundance.*
> *I am a spark of light.*
> *I am loving and generous.*
> *I am a positive influence on everything and everyone*
>   *around me.*
> *I bring light to every situation.*
> *Every person I meet has a gift to offer.*
> *I have integrity, dignity, and strength.*
> *I am a creative, interesting person.*
> *I am secure and at peace.*
> *I love and am loved.*
> *Today is full of hope.*
> *I am intelligent and creative.*
> *I am strong mentally and physically.*
> *I love the people around me.*
> *I am confident and at ease in all situations.*

Every situation brings me opportunities to discover
more of my power, creativity, skill, and talent.
There are sources of support around and within me.
All things are possible.

You now have a place to begin to create the higher ideals you want to make a part of your thinking. You can develop many strengths within yourself through affirming positive thoughts. Listening to sacred music, reading poetry, reciting inspirational verse or prose will help you to envision yourself as an elightened being. You will discover that you can cultivate more often and more regularly those experiences of awe and revelation. As your imagination expands, you will elevate your state of awareness and look forward to each day for the opportunity it brings.

Becoming Empowered

Within each one of us there resides a spark of life, an inner urge to create, a drive to improve, expand, and multiply. We may perceive this as a desire to make a difference in the world, to leave a mark, to touch people, to influence the environment in a productive way, or simply a desire for self expression.

Every time we create—whether it is a work of art, piece of music, healthy relationship, physical object, business venture—we become more aware of our creative power. We come closer to understanding creation through the creative act. The world in which we live is a beautiful place. It is full of resources—people and places and things for us to use, to enjoy, to share, to explore, and to discover. Life is designed for us to live. Too many people waste this precious gift of life by merely struggling to survive. What's the point? Why struggle to feed the body when there is no time left for appreciating a beautiful sunset, for sharing a tender moment with a child, for receiving the awe of a Mozart sonata?

Using visualization with control will give you command of your life. It will give you the freedom you were designed to have. We each have the ability to image and we each have free will. This means that we have freedom when we create responsibly. We are responsible for our creations; we experience their effects and it is our duty to use this schoolroom called life for learning and understanding. When we do create with purpose, when we strive to improve ourselves and to develop our full potential, we can experience a life full of riches and power.

When we forget that we are creative and live only according to habit or only by repeating the past, we experience limitation and stagnation. This produces the struggle for survival. When you find yourself "stuck," unhappy, limited, or victimized by conditions in your life, ask yourself, "Who is controlling my life?" To whom are you giving up your power? Nobody can make you think a certain way or make your choices for you; it is always in your hands and in your mind to choose for yourself how to think, how to act, how to live. It is in your hands and intelligence to cause and create your own life.

Physical conditions do not cause you to be who you are. When you think this way you become entrapped in limitations. Listen to your thoughts. When you think, "I can't help it, I'm only human," "I just didn't have any choice," "I can't do anything about it," you are entrapped in your own limitations. You are denying the creative power of your mind. When you think that other people "make you" happy or sad, when your financial situation "causes" you to miss out on something you want to do or when you feel trapped by any situation, you stagnate by refusing to imagine and cause change. You are a victim of other people, conditions or circumstances when you allow your mind to remain passive.

Some people interpret this to mean that when things are not going well it is their fault. "I'm not to blame for my car breaking down!" Please understand that "cause" and "blame" are not synonymous. I do not believe that anyone intentionally creates disasters in his or her life! I do believe that people are ignorant of how to use their mind power effectively. Learn to forgive yourself for the conditions that displease you and then do something different. Learn how to listen to your thoughts so that you can identify the ways of thinking that contribute to your poverty, or illness, or whatever limitation you face. Then, use visualization to cause change.

If you find that you repeatedly set up conditions in your life in which you are limited or feel like a victim, some form of counseling may help you to discover the cause in your thinking. As a counselor, I have found that people who have difficulty admitting their participation in such situations describe them using the word "you" instead of "I." For example, I was counseling a woman I will call Carol. She was very promiscuous and kept getting involved with men who treated her poorly. She was describing how her mother embarassed her when she started developing a woman's body in adolescence. Her mother was afraid that Carol would get hurt by boys and so she deliberately had Carol wear clothes that were unflattering to ward off any male attention. As Carol described it, she said, "you feel really bad when your mother wants you to look ugly." By speaking this way, Carol removed herself from the situation rather than claiming her own feelings, "*I* felt really bad because my mother wanted me to look ugly." Gradually, she started admitting how she felt and the choices she made as a result. She had purposely chosen to run around with many men to prove to herself that she was an attractive woman. By admitting her desire for importance, value and worth, she gained some perspective on her reason for making these choices. This was very empowering, because it helped her to realize that she had chosen to defy her mother in an attempt to assert her own worth but the final result perpetuated her thoughts of worthlessness. Carol's actions were similar to those her mother had chosen when she was an adolescent and it was those very actions her mother wanted to protect Carol from experiencing. Once Carol faced her own desires and admitted how she set up these situations herself, she was free to cause change. She started imagining different ways to give as a way to develop self value. She became a teacher, helping children learn and grow, and as Carol experienced a positive influence in their lives she found out that she was a good person. She started making different choices in her relationships with men, no longer craving their attention to know that she was worthwhile. Through creative imagery Carol broke a "dysfunctional" family pattern. She learned to understand her own motives and imagined a different way of living to fulfill her desire.

In most cases, when you think in limited ways, it is because you have been taught this. Perhaps, as a child, someone told you, "You will never amount to anything." "The Joneses have always been poor, and you are no exception," or something else that you accepted and believed. Your parents are not to blame. They gave you what they knew, and you responded according to your understanding at the time. Do not dwell in the past. You may want to receive counseling to look for the cause of unproductive ways of thinking. This means discovering how and when you began forming certain attitudes that have limited you, not pointing the finger at someone else who destroyed your life. *You* accepted the unproductive attitudes, *you* imaged them, and *you* have practiced them. The power to change is therefore in your hands. Whatever you have imagined about yourself you have created in your life. You have repeated it through habit and practice. Because you have imagined yourself to be a certain way, you can also imagine yourself to be a different way. What freedom! You can choose how to think and what to imagine! Examine your thoughts and decide which ones are productive and useful to you and which are not. Change the ones that are not useful to thoughts which will produce your desires.

You may have difficulty imagining the prosperity, success, or conditions you desire. In this case, use role models. Find people who live the kind of lifestyle you would desire for yourself. Look for people who exhibit qualities and traits you want to emulate. Real people, fictional characters, and historical figures all can provide a stimulus for your imagination. Research, read, and meet people. Craft an image that is appealing to you. Then, image *yourself* being like the people that you admire. The more you imagine yourself in this way, the more you will become like that.

When you realize that you always have the ability to choose the thoughts you desire, you become empowered. Will power is a series of continuous, unceasing, undiscourageable efforts and actions focused around a desire. Making consistent choices in the direction of your desire will produce the change you want. When you recognize that you have been practicing a negative way of thinking, appreciate your ability to be aware of your thoughts, and visualize something else. Do not become discouraged, keep practicing to visualize the way of thinking that will produce success. Practice makes perfect. It is important to remember that "perfection" is not a stagnant state. Often people will put off acting on a desire because they fear they will not be perfect at accomplishing it. Achieving perfection in every activity means doing your best, striving to become better and to improve and grow and learn. Recently I watched an insect called a walking stick climbing over a leaf. It kept falling, then it would turn itself upright and move again. It kept going until it finally got to the top surface of the leaf. The leaves on the ground were many different shades of green, brown, gold and scarlet. Some were spotted, some irregularly-shaped, some even appeared torn. Each leaf or bug or bird in nature is individual — some graceful, some awkward, some straight, some bent, some fast, some slow — each one just *is* what it is. All are moving toward something and each makes up a part of the whole. Imagine if all human beings developed a self concept like this. We could release thoughts of condemnation and appreciate the diversity of life. We could embrace the changes and stages of learning and growth.

As long as you blame other people or conditions outside of you for the situations in your life, you will feel weak and helpless. You cannot change someone else. But you *can* change yourself. Admitting that *you are the cause* for your life will bring to you a great awareness of your power. When you understand that "cause" means command, you will cease blaming yourself for the conditions you don't like. You will respect your ability *to cause* and simply direct your thinking in a new way to visualize the conditions and circumstances you want. A simple place to practice this kind of command is in relationships with other people. Most of us have been taught in some way to blame other people for our own thoughts, feelings, or conditions. "Oh, she makes me feel so good," we say when we're in love. "He drives me crazy," when we're angry. Another person can stimulate you, can bring to your attention your own thoughts and feelings, but they do not put these thoughts or feelings in your mind. When you understand that they bring to your attention what is already within you, you have a great amount of freedom. You can always choose your response to another individual.

If you feel good in the presence of another person, identify what it is about them that you like. List the qualities you find pleasing. Describe what they stimulate within you. Perhaps you find them funny, warm, affectionate, friendly, and compassionate. Look to see how many of these qualities you practice yourself. When you are actively building these attributes within your own being you will be at ease with the other person. You will be free to speak your mind and to be yourself. If you do not make these a part of you, most likely you will become dependent on that other person to "fill in" these missing qualities in yourself. You may find yourself "irresistibly" drawn to them. You may drop other important activities in your life to be in the presence of your beloved. In that case, you will probably try to make that person your goal. You may attempt to build your life around them. A popular song by the group Fleetwood Mac describes the anguish of putting another person in the position to direct your own life, "I've been so afraid of changing/ 'Cause I've built my life around you/ But time makes you bolder, even children get older/ And I'm getting older too."

Caution! You cannot make another person your goal. People change. People have free will. To create healthy relationships means having individuals who are strong and have a clear sense of their own identity with their own goals. The mutual ideals they share form the basis of the relationship. When you do not have this as a point of reference, you will find yourself feeling controlled by the other person, or reacting to the other person because you will see them as the cause for your happiness or unhappiness. While you may depend on them to make decisions for you, you will also resent it when their choices determine the course of your life. This leads to the eventual deterioration and destruction of the relationship. Decide who *you* want to be and practice being that. Create yourself as the ideal mate, partner, or friend that you want to be. Bring to the relationship your best Self so that you are contributing rather than trying to take something from your partner. Visualize how you want to communicate, to be intimate, to express the qualities you desire. Image the conditions you want in your association. Visualize yourself being open, loving, compassionate, generous, strong-willed or however else you want to be. Do not try to visualize the other person as you want them to be, for you will only be setting yourself up for failure. Respect their right to choose and to be the individual they are.

This doesn't mean that you have to be a passive victim. If there is something that displeases you about the other person, communicate. But — and this is *very important* — communicate from the perspective of what *you* want and what *you* think and feel. Do not blame the other person for making you angry, or unhappy, etc. Use "I" statements to describe your experience. This will give you the awareness of how *you* think and will give you the perspective of how much freedom you have to choose what to do in the situation. You will understand yourself, your motives and your intentions in this way and will be able to perceive your partner clearly.

For example, let's say you have a partner who demands a lot of attention from you. They are jealous, and when you spend time with your friends they pout to get your attention. Suppose you have lived with this for awhile, you have stewed about it, and now you are angry. Instead of blasting your partner with accusations like, "You make me so angry! You're such a baby! You have no reason to be jealous," which will only provoke defensiveness, give yourself some credit for what you experience. "I feel isolated from you and I want to talk with you. I want to be close with you and I get angry with you when I think I can't. I feel pulled in two directions when I want to see my friends and I know you feel neglected. I am unhappy when you are pouting because I want to grow with you." This is more honest, describes your feelings, and lets the other person know what your perspective is. Then they can respond with what they think and feel. Rather than, "You don't care about me. You care more about your friends than me," they can say, "I want your attention and I feel lonely when you are out with your friends." These kinds of statements will open lines of communication that will lead to great discoveries of your thoughts, attitudes and the feelings that result as well as the thoughts and attitudes and feelings of your partner. You will know what you want and what your partner wants, and vice versa. It will aid you to respect and love one another. You will discover that you always have the freedom to change how you think about one another and to create better ways of relating with one another.

You can practice this kind of communication with any-one — your children, spouse, boss, friends, or parents. You will find tremendous freedom and power as you own your thoughts. You will discover that every thought and reaction is of your own making, and you can shape your thinking as you desire. Living your life will become a creative art. Just as a sculptor molds clay or a painter puts brush to canvas, you can form the attitudes, actions and responses that express your ideal self. You can alter these at any time to create the *you* that is most fulfilling and desirable. No matter what conditions life brings your way, you are free to respond and change and move your own destiny.

Being responsible for yourself and your creations means that you respond to your desires with action. When you desire something, whether it is a new pair of shoes or a more honest relationship, the power is in your hands to create it. As long as you think that someone else is pulling your strings, they will be. When you practice creating what you want, causing change with your visualized thought forms and accompanying actions, you will find that your experiences are unlimited. Your ability to change is never ending. And your awareness of yourself and your relationship with all of creation will expand to heights greater than ever before.

The following points will help you to admit your power:

1. Thoughts are things and everything is created with thought.

2. You are a mental-spiritual being and your physical experiences are for your learning.

3. The secret to visualization is creating clear, detailed thought forms using all five senses.

4. You must release your visualized thought form to your subconscious mind for manifestation.

5. The language of mind is in pictures or images.

6. You have free will; therefore, you always have the freedom to choose the thoughts you want to think and create.

7. Other people have free will. You can create *yourself* as you desire but you cannot create someone else.

8. The physical world, your physical body, physical conditions will respond to the direction of your thoughts.

9. Thought directed with intelligence is the greatest power in the universe.

10. You are endowed with imagination and will; therefore, creating and fulfilling desires is inherent in your nature.

11. Like attracts like. Therefore, create positively and with love.

12. Love is the magnetic attraction between positive and negative poles. Be aggressive by shaping the thought images you desire and receptive by expecting and watching for your desires to come to you.

13. The nature of matter is change. If you don't like something in your life, you can change it to become what you want. Imagining how you want to improve yourself and conditions in your life is the first step in making it so.

14. You have the freedom to choose your response to any person, place, or thing in your life. Love your enemies by creating understanding. When you initiate the response you desire, you have the power of understanding, which produces inner and outer peace.

15. When you feel trapped in any limitation, imagine every alternative you can think of. When you have exhausted the probabilities you can imagine, start imagining possibilities. Remember that you can always add to what you have and what you experience by imagining "what if...?"

16. When using creative imagery, craft your desires with *Ideal* (what you want), *Purpose* (why you want it, who you will become in the process of creating it), and *Activity* (the steps of mental and physical preparation—the "how to.") This formula insures your success.

I hope that you will use this book to create the life you desire. As you come to a greater understanding of your creative power, share your discoveries with others. When you aid others to abundance, you will have abundance yourself. When we are all fulfilling the innermost desires of our souls, the world will be a better place.

I give you my circle of love.

About the Author

All of her life Laurel Jan Fuller has embraced the pursuit of education. Born in Denver, Colorado and reared in Mount Vernon, New York, Laurel excelled in academics graduating valedictorian of her high school class. She is a Phi Beta Kappa graduate of the University of Michigan with a Bachelor of Arts in Women's Studies.

Taught from a young age the value of a well-rounded education, Laurel learned to play the piano and studied literature, philosophy, Jungian psychology, languages, theater and other liberal arts. During her college years her open-minded inquisitiveness prompted her to practice transcendental meditation, study martial arts with a Zen master and yoga at an ashram. Seeking an even deeper understanding of Universal Truth, in 1979 Laurel began her formal study of metaphysics through the School of Metaphysics. She has received the first two degrees offered by the School and is currently completing requirements for her Doctorate in Metaphysics. She holds a Doctorate in Divinity and is a certified psi counselor.

The urge to share her wisdom with others has been an integral part of her life, from her early years as a tutor in elementary and high school to a teaching assistant and facilitator in college. She has been a faculty member of the School of Metaphysics since 1979. Laurel has served humanity in many capacities through this non-profit organization for the past fifteen years and is currently the National Vice President. An accomplished speaker, she lectures throughout the United States to universities, corporations and professional organizations. Senior Editor of *Thresholds Quarterly*, poet, and lyricist, Laurel appreciates the written and spoken word as a vehicle for bringing Truth to humanity.

Additional titles available through SOM Publising include:

Permanent Healing
Dr. Daniel R. Condron   ISBN 0944386-12-1 $9.95

Dreams of the Soul - The Yogi Sutras of Patanjali
Dr. Daniel R. Condron   ISBN 0944386-11-3 $9.95

TOTAL RECALL -
An Introduction to Past Life & Health Readings
Dr. Barbara Condron, ed. ISBN 0944386-10-5 $9.95

Kundalini Rising - Mastering Your Creative Energies
Dr. Barbara Condron   ISBN 0944386-13-X $9.95

Going in Circles - Search for a Satisfying Relationship
Dr. Barbara Condron   ISBN 0944386-00-8 $5.95

What Will I Do Tomorrow? Probing Depression
Dr. Barbara Condron   ISBN 0944386-02-4 $4.95

Who Were Those Strangers in My Dream?
Dr. Barbara Condron   ISBN 0944386-08-3 $4.95

Meditation: Answer to Your Prayers by Dr. Jerry L. Rothermel
ISBN 0944386-01-6 $4.95

Dreams: Language of the Soul by Dr. Jerry L. Rothermel
ISBN 0944386-04-0 $4.95

Symbols of Dreams by Dr. Jerry L. Rothermel
ISBN 0944386-03-2 $4.95

Mechanics of Dreams by Dr. Jerry L. Rothermel
ISBN 0944386-09-1 $6.95

HuMan, a novel by Dr. Jerry L. Rothermel
ISBN 0944386-05-9 $5.95

Discovering the Kingdom of Heaven by Dr. Gayle B. Matthes
ISBN 0944386-07-5 $5.95

Autobiography of a Skeptic by Frank Farmer
ISBN 0944386-06-7 $7.95

To order, or for a catalogue of all titles available, write:
SOM Publishing
School of Metaphysics
National Headquarters
Windyville, Missouri 65783
Enclose a check or money order payable to SOM with any order.
Please include $2.00 for postage and handling of books.

About the School of Metaphysics

We invite you to become a special part of our efforts to aid in enhancing and quickening the process of spiritual growth and mental evolution of the people of the world. The School of Metaphysics, a not-for-profit educational and service organization, has been in existence for more than two decades. During that time, we have taught tens of thousands directly through our course of study in applied metaphysics. We have elevated the awareness of millions through the many services we offer. If you would like to pursue the study of the mind and the transformation of Self to a higher level of being and consciousness, you are invited to write to us at the School of Metaphysics National Headquarters in Windyville, Missouri 65783.

The heart of the School of Metaphysics is a three-tiered program of study. Lessons introduce you to the Universal Laws and Truths which guide spiritual and physical evolution. Consciousness is explored and developed through mental and spiritual disciplines which enhance your physical life and enrich your soul progression. We teach concentration, visualization (focused imagery), meditation, and control of life force and creative energies. As a student, you will develop an understanding of the purpose of life and your purpose for this lifetime.

Experts in the language of the mind, we teach how to remember and understand the inner communication received through dreams. We are the sponsors of the National Dream Hotline® an *annual educational service offered the last week-end in April. Study centers are located throughout the Midwest. If there is not a center near you, you can receive the first series of lessons through corre-spondence with a teacher at our headquarters.*

There is the opportunity *to aid in the growth and fulfillment of our work. Donations are accepted and are a valuable way for you to aid humanity by supporting the expansion of the School of Metaphysics' efforts. Currently, donations are being received for Project Octagon, the first educa-tional building on the College of Metaphysics campus. The land for the proposed campus is located in the beautiful Ozark Mountains of Mis-souri, three hours from St. Louis and Kansas City, and one hour north of Springfield. The four-story octagon design will enable us to increase head-quarters staff and enrollment in our College work/ study program. This proposed multi-purpose structure will include an auditorium, classrooms, library and study areas, a cafeteria, and potential living quarters for up to 100 people. We expect to finance this structure through corporate grants and personal endowments. Gifts may be named for the donor or be designated as an ongoing memorial fund to a family member or special friend. Dona-tions to the School of Metaphysics are tax-exempt under 501 (c) (3) of the Internal Revenue Code. We appreciate any contribution you are free to make. With the help of people like you, our dream of a place where anyone desiring Self awareness can receive wholistic education will become a reality.*

We send you our Circle of Love.